Shatterhand
Massacree

Shatterhand Massacree

AND OTHER MEDIA TEXTS

John Jesurun

New York, New York

Shatterhand Massacree and Other Media Texts is published by PAJ Publications, P.O. Box 532, Village Station, New York, NY 10014.

PAJ Publications is distributed to the trade by Consortium Book Sales and Distribution: www.cbsd.com

Publisher of PAJ Publications: Bonnie Marranca

 This publication is made possible with public funds from the New York State Council on the Arts, a state agency.

Library of Congress Cataloging-in-Publication Data

Jesurun, John.
  Shatterhand massacree and other media texts / John Jesurun.
     p. cm.
  ISBN 978-1-55554-084-5
  I. Title.

PS3610.E877S53 2009
812'.6—dc22

                         2008055688

First Edition, 2009
Printed in the United States of America

Contents

Acknowledgments

I would like to thank the following individuals and institutions for their support of my work: Ellen Stewart, La MaMa, Danspace, Richard Connors, Familia Jesurun, Paula Court, Mickery Theater, Ritsaert ten Cate, The Rockefeller Foundation, The Kitchen, The MacDowell Colony, The Flintridge Foundation, The Peg Santvoord Foundation, Hallwalls, Steve Gallagher, Randolph St. Gallery, Mike Taylor, Frank Maya, Ben Geffen, Dan Lee, BAM/Lucent Arts in Multimedia, Tim Coulter, Zishan Ugurlu, Dance Theater Workshop, Andrzej Wirth, Rebecca Moore, Dayton Taylor, Jeff Nash, Carla Peterson, Kit August, Eugene Lang College/The New School, Franklin Furnace Fund, Jennifer Ortega, New City Theater, Bill Ballou, U.S./Mexico Fund. Special thanks to Bonnie Marranca of PAJ Publications for taking on this project.

Shatterhand Massacree

Shatterhand Massacree was first performed at St. Mark's Church, Danspace Project, New York City, November 1985.

Cast

MOTHER: Sanghi Wagner
FATHER: Larry Tighe
SON: Steve Buscemi
DAUGHTER: Valerie Charles
BOY: Michael Tighe

Brad Philips: *Stage Manager*
Carol Mullins: *Lighting Design*

Directed and designed by John Jesurun

Four television monitors, each upturned vertically, sit on four-foot-high pedestals. Each monitor plays the same loop of an open window with a curtain blowing in the breeze. Two monitors sit at either side of the edge of the stage, and two sit side by side at the center rear of the stage. A rectangular table with a white top sits center stage. Three chairs surround it. Two more chairs sit at either side of the front of the stage facing each other.

FATHER, MOTHER, DAUGHTER *sit at table.* SON *sits on chair at right end of stage.*

MOTHER: You are asleep, but you are flying, but you are not a wolf.

FATHER: You're going on a journey, a vacation.

MOTHER: But there will be no sharks.

FATHER: No wolves.

MOTHER: Just clouds like rock formations.

DAUGHTER: A cloud is a rock formation that has fainted.

FATHER: OK?

SON: OK, Daddy.

MOTHER: Tell me about the horse.

DAUGHTER: The horse was masked, the horse was asked, the rider was gone, there never was any rider or any reindeer, and the horse was attracted to the reindeer. The rider was attracted to the horse. Is that correct?

FATHER: And we prosecuted correctly.

DAUGHTER: Where were we going? I don't know. We were masked, and they put us in here.

MOTHER: I took your word for it that you knew where we were going; but you didn't know.

FATHER: But the screen kiss, the world's longest screen kiss.

SON: Oh, screen kiss, screen kiss, there was no screen kiss.

DAUGHTER: Hey, your cigarette's burning up.

MOTHER: As I remember it, the publicity blurbs described it as the longest screen kiss in history.

FATHER: As a matter of fact, the actors hated doing it. They felt terribly uncomfortable at the way in which they had to cling to each other. I said, "I don't care how you feel. The only thing that matters is how it's going to look on the screen."

DAUGHTER: I imagine the reader will want to know why these two professionals were so ill at ease during this scene. To be specific, there was a close-up on their two faces together as they moved across the whole set. The problem for them was how to walk across glued to each other in that way; while the only thing that concerned you was to show their faces together on the screen.

FATHER: Oh, for heaven's sake.

SON: I don't feel well.

FATHER: Exactly. I conceived that scene in terms of the participants' desire not to—

MOTHER:—interrupt the romantic moment. We live in this house.

DAUGHTER: The last thing that we remember is that we fell asleep, and then the house started to spin like in a hurricane, and the Wizard of Oz and the Wiz went by the witch, and a tree, and a car, and a windmill, and too many fish.

SON: Fish.

FATHER: And the whole sea went by.

DAUGHTER: And a whole sky, and southern skies, and clouds.

MOTHER: We were jet-propelled home, but we were in our own home.

FATHER: We landed on a runway.

DAUGHTER: It gave me the heebie-jeebies to think about it, so we drank water and forgot about it.

FATHER: Then we clashed with the ground.

Cut. Blackout.

FATHER, MOTHER, DAUGHTER sit at table eating. They use black arrows as forks.

FATHER: There it is.

DAUGHTER: Where?

MOTHER: On your plate.

DAUGHTER: Oh yes, there it is.

FATHER: Do you hear hammering?

MOTHER: No.

FATHER: I hear a knocking.

MOTHER: No.

FATHER: Someone knocking from somewhere.

DAUGHTER: How could there be a knocking?

FATHER: A ticking.

MOTHER: Have some more.

DAUGHTER: Thanks.

FATHER: What is this?

DAUGHTER: Oh really, it's great.

MOTHER: I am the one who cooked it.

DAUGHTER: Eels in eel broth, mother. Eels in eels broth, mother.

FATHER: Is that what you had at your friend's house?

DAUGHTER: Yes.

FATHER: Tell us the story about the idiot king.

DAUGHTER: The idiot king of Ohio, or Wyoming?

MOTHER: Wyoming.

DAUGHTER: There once was a king of Wyoming.

FATHER: And he was an idiot …

DAUGHTER: But it didn't matter.

MOTHER: Why?

DAUGHTER: Because he was happy.

FATHER: He was an idiot but …

MOTHER: How could he be happy?

DAUGHTER: Because he didn't have to think about anything; he just was an idiot. And he was so happy

because he didn't have to think about anything or worry. But then one day they came to kill him.

FATHER: Because …

DAUGHTER: Because they thought one day he'd smarten up, and then they'd have—

MOTHER:—trouble in the house.

DAUGHTER: But he was such an idiot that he didn't know they were trying to kill and he got away by mistake, and all the killers fell into a lake and were eaten and bitten by vampires;. but he didn't even notice because he was such an idiot. And so he continued—

FATHER:—being an idiot, and he was so happy.

MOTHER: I love that story.

FATHER: Tell the one about the horse.

MOTHER: No, not that one.

FATHER: Tell us the one about the horse.

MOTHER: No, not that one.

FATHER: Not that one at night.

MOTHER: Have some more horseshoe crab.

DAUGHTER: Thanks.

MOTHER: What's that bending?

DAUGHTER: No bending.

MOTHER: Yes, the fence out there is bending.

FATHER: In the wind. The wind is getting strong.

MOTHER: It used to be just wispy this afternoon, and now it's bending strong.

FATHER: Close the window. Thank you.

MOTHER: Close the window.

DAUGHTER: All right.

FATHER: And turn out the lights and listen. (Father stands behind Daughter and holds her arms out.)

MOTHER: There were dim blue lights in the foreground, the chair was cold, and the letters were big.

DAUGHTER: The letters were big, right, Daddy? Right.

FATHER: They had recently begun putting together the arms of the Venus de Mislan. They'd found them in a box shattered into thousands and thousands of pieces. It took them twenty-five years to assemble them, and when they finally put them together again, they were the wrong arms. The time and money—apparently forty thousand dollars and hours in researchers' and craftsmen's fees over the years.

MOTHER: The man who investigated the reconstruction was so furious that he became drunk one evening and in a rage broke them into twice as many pieces as they were to begin with—eighty thousand. He later lost his job and disappeared after a long vacation. That was my father.

FATHER: Her father. How does it feel to have such an illustrious Father?

MOTHER: I never knew him.

DAUGHTER: You didn't ?

MOTHER: No. I was born just before he went on vacation.

DAUGHTER: Where did he go?

FATHER: Greece.

DAUGHTER: Oh, how lovely.

MOTHER: Nothing about that vacation he took is lovely to me.

FATHER: Well, let's talk about something else.

DAUGHTER: I'm sorry if I've upset you.

MOTHER: You have.

FATHER: Forget it. It's all in the past.

DAUGHTER: All in the past, all in the past, that's what you always say.

FATHER: That's what I always say.

MOTHER: Can't you stop saying it?

FATHER: What else can I say?

MOTHER: Nothing.

FATHER: Then I'll say nothing.

MOTHER: And please don't bring up Papa again. It's just too sad and embarrassing to hear that story and know it was my father.

DAUGHTER: Those poor arms.

MOTHER: Go to sleep.

FATHER: Goodnight.

Cut. Blackout.

FATHER, MOTHER, DAUGHTER at table.

FATHER: What can I say?

DAUGHTER: Where is my brother?

MOTHER: The son that no one talks about. Reynardine, a small vampire wolf-boy.

DAUGHTER: Never talk about him.

FATHER: Because he's gone and taken away.

DAUGHTER: Poor vampire boy.

MOTHER: It wasn't his fault.

FATHER: He was a small vampire, and he couldn't stop talking about love.

MOTHER: It would have just caused problems later on.

DAUGHTER: Well, he's coming back. I called him.

MOTHER: Your twin brother.

FATHER: But he doesn't look like me; he looks like you.

MOTHER: Yes.

DAUGHTER: Poor vampire boy.

FATHER: I told her not to call him.

DAUGHTER: He'll arrive.

MOTHER: You'll be sorry.

DAUGHTER: He won't hurt us.

MOTHER: He doesn't mean to bite.

Father: Call the police.

Mother: They won't involve themselves.

Father: What will we do?

Mother: Just wait.

Daughter: I'm not afraid.

Mother: He would stand next to the fire and sing.

Father: Weird songs.

Daughter: They were nice songs.

Mother: Pretty.

Father: Songs about burning.

Daughter: Songs about flying.

Mother: I'm glad he's coming back.

Father: I'm not.

Mother: He should be here any minute.

Daughter: Would he like some supper? You'll see, he'll be harmless.

Mother: We're not afraid.

Father: Yes we are.

Daughter: He'd sing songs by the fire.

Father: Songs about burning.

Mother: Songs about flying and love.

Daughter: You think he's scary, but he's not. He never was.

Father: We have to be careful.

Daughter: He doesn't bite.

Father: You don't know him.

Cut. Blackout.

MOTHER and DAUGHTER at table. FATHER sits on chair stage right. SON stands stage left.

FATHER: Good morning.

MOTHER: How long has it been?

SON: Seven years.

DAUGHTER: At least.

MOTHER: It's been a seven-year ache. We missed you.

SON: (Holds black arrow. Begins to circle table.) You never missed me.

FATHER: You look so much like me.

SON: I am you.

FATHER: You are not me.

SON: I am you. That's why you can't look at me.

FATHER: I'm not you.

MOTHER: He's not you.

DAUGHTER: Is he you, Daddy?

FATHER: You hate me.

SON: I love you even though you sent me away.

FATHER: You've got a strange kind of love.

SON: Not strange.

FATHER: It's like burning.

SON: Not burning.

FATHER: Strange.

SON: Not so strange. I remember that vacation. *(Standing in front of FA-THER, he points arrow at him.)*

FATHER: Don't talk about that vacation.

SON: I remember that vacation. It began at a beautiful island resort in Mexico, incredibly bluey water.

Bright clear skies, bright white beaches. The houses were all modernistic, dark red cubist architecture.

Right? *(He stands behind table.)*

MOTHER: You'd like a scotch. I'll fix it.

SON: There was iron work, modern, split-level. All the servants were not Mexican. For some reason they

wore Greek robes. They carried spears in one hand while they carried the trays. Right?

FATHER: He's not thirsty.

SON: I was parched. So we walk down to the beach. Bright colors. I look closer, and the water seems to

have a strange film on it, and in the shallow water are these strange rubber-like plants washed up from the

bottom of the sea. Right?

DAUGHTER: We poked at them.

SON: They also seem like animals, but they puzzled us. They're dead. Also the water seems very warm.

Ugh, we say, we can't go into that and that weird film on the water. So we walked a little further, and we come upon a huge dead black shark washed up on shore. We notice huge sharks in the water swimming in circles. We shouted for the people in the water to get out. They don't see the sharks. The sharks begin to attack them. We scream and try to help them out.

FATHER: Don't listen to him; it never happened that way.

SON: Some people were bitten. *(Motioning with arrow.)* A huge helicopter appears in the right-hand corner. It is so big we can't even see it all. It flies so low we think it's going to hit the water. We think …

FATHER: It never happened that way. Cover your ears. We think it hits the water, but actually it's a huge wave coming up.

MOTHER: You're trying to scare us. Go back inside.

SON: … between us and the helicopter obscuring it in such a way that we think it's gone under. The waves recede, and the helicopter is safe, although it's still flying very low, and we signal to it to go away because of the sharks. It comes really close to the water, and a huge shark as big as a blimp jumps out at it. And so do the other sharks. The big one flips over it and weighs it down so much that it comes crashing down into the water. *(He hits the table with the point of the arrow and it drops.)* We scream. By this time the sharks are gigantic and have turned into cartoon shapes, although they are real. I feel a huge cramp in my right leg. I wake up with a terrible cramp in my right leg, which I fight really hard. I try to pull the muscle the other way, but the cramp won't give in. I keep pulling, but the cramp is pulling too hard, like it has a will of its own, so I let it have its own way. *(Blackout.)* It's so dark in here.

FATHER: No it's not.

SON: Yes it is.

DAUGHTER: Yes it is.

FATHER: I told you not to listen to him.

MOTHER: It is not dark.

SON: It is dark.

DAUGHTER: It's a hurricane, a prairie fire.

"Hey, Bulldog" instrumental music loop by The Beatles begins. SON and DAUGHTER dance on table top in dim light.

FATHER and MOTHER run around the table in circles.

FATHER: Stop it, stop it, stop doing that.

MOTHER: Stop that dancing. If you must do it, do it outside.

Son and Daughter scream and bark.

FATHER: Stop it. *(FATHER barks.)* Stop.

Cut. Blackout.

SON lying on table, face up. MOTHER, DAUGHTER, FATHER lean over him.

DAUGHTER: *(Her ear to SON's chest.)* Listen to the rhythm of his heart.

FATHER: There is no heartbeat.

DAUGHTER: There has to be.

MOTHER: No heartbeat.

DAUGHTER: Does that mean he's not alive?

MOTHER: Of course not.

FATHER: It's just not beating.

DAUGHTER: Dance! *(Still lying down, SON begins dance movements.)* He can't be dead if he's dancing.

FATHER: A ghost dance.

DAUGHTER: Ghosts don't dance like that.

MOTHER: It doesn't matter if the heart beats or not. He's dancing anyway.

FATHER: Forget it.

DAUGHTER: Forget it, he's fine.

MOTHER: Who cares if the heart's beating or not?

DAUGHTER: It's just out for a while. It'll come back in. Stop dancing. (Son becomes still.) Now listen. It's beating. Just had to get into shape. If you feel it stop again, just start dancing.

SON: Sure.

Cut. Blackout. "Hey, Bulldog" music returns.

FATHER, MOTHER, DAUGHTER sit at table eating with arrows. SON sits on chair at right side of stage.

MOTHER: I can hear a bird singing far away. A mouse chirping.

DAUGHTER: I hear the hens talking at night in the hen house. They say, "Now tomorrow we'll go back to Denmark."

FATHER: Uh-huh, yes, sure.

DAUGHTER: A hen's trip to Denmark.

SON: Or a snowball in hell.

DAUGHTER: Or the pope in hell.

SON: Hey, there's a lot of popes in hell.

FATHER: Really the soup is good.

SON: I taste dirt in my nose and throat.

MOTHER: When you fell off that swing you had a mouth full of dirt.

DAUGHTER: That's what it is.

SON: Don't tell me.

MOTHER: Don't talk about Jesus.

FATHER: How long are you staying?

SON: I'm staying.

FATHER: You're ghoulish.

SON: You're ghoulish.

DAUGHTER: Who was that riderless horse anyway?

MOTHER: I don't know.

SON: Some lonely bluesman.

FATHER: With a bottleneck slide guitar.

MOTHER: No guitar.

SON: Lord, I wish I was catfish dancing in the deep blue sea.

DAUGHTER: I'd have all the good-lookin' men fishin' after me.

FATHER: You watch out.

SON: What is this food?

FATHER: Eels.

SON: Oh Lord.

FATHER: Don't talk about Jesus

SON: The Bible says Jesus was half-man and half-wolf.

DAUGHTER: Forever and ever.

MOTHER: *Siempre.*

DAUGHTER: It means always.

FATHER: In Spanish.

DAUGHTER: Always.

SON: Forever and ever.

FATHER: Where have you been?

DAUGHTER: *Loco.*

SON: *Loco en cabeza.*

DAUGHTER: It means crazy in head in Spanish.

FATHER: Where have you been, my wolf-boy son?

MOTHER: Where have you been, my handsome young one?

SON: I've been with my sweetheart, Mother. Oh, make my bed soon for I'm sick to the heart and I'll faint, what'll I do?

FATHER: What did she give you for supper, my wolf-boy son?

MOTHER: What did she give you for supper, my handsome young one?

SON: Eels in eel broth, mother. Eels in eel broth, mother. Make my bed soon, I'm sick to the heart and I'll faint, what'll I do?

FATHER: What color were the skins, my wolf-boy son?

MOTHER: What color were the skins, my handsome young one ?

SON: Brown and speckled, mother. Brown and speckled, mother. Make my bed soon, I'm sick to the heart and I'll faint, what'll I do?

FATHER: I think you've been poisoned, my wolf-boy son.

MOTHER: I think you've been poisoned, my handsome young one.

SON: Oh yes, and I'm dead, Mother. Make my bed soon, I'm sick to the heart and I'll faint, what'll I do?

MOTHER: What will you leave your mother, my wolf-boy son?

SON: My gold and silver, mother, make my bed soon, what'll I do?

FATHER: What will you leave your father, my wolf-boy son?

SON: A rope from hell to hang him. A rope from hell to hang him! *(Breaks arrow over knee and tosses pieces away. He walks to stand in front of FA-THER.)* Make my bed soon, I'm sick to the heart and I'll faint, what'll I do?!

FATHER: He has to leave. *(FATHER and SON begin walking in circles around the table in opposite directions.)*

DAUGHTER: Why?

MOTHER: He sends a pressure from down there.

FATHER: Where all the resources are.

DAUGHTER: When did he leave?

FATHER: He was four.

MOTHER: And now he's ten.

FATHER: We sent him away.

MOTHER: He ran away.

FATHER: He was killing everything.

MOTHER: The plants, the animals on the farm.

FATHER: He had to go.

MOTHER: So he ran away.

FATHER: And we said he died.

MOTHER: A vampire wolf-boy.

FATHER: A wolf in his heart. What could we have done? He would have
    ended up amoral, violent, bestial, an animal machine.

DAUGHTER: Does he think he's a wolf?

MOTHER: Ask him.

SON: I am not a wolf.

DAUGHTER: He is not a wolf.

FATHER: Wait until nightfall.

SON: Daddy, I am not a wolf.

FATHER: Then where did the shark story come from?

SON: Our vacation. I am not a vampire wolf.

DAUGHTER: Or if you are, then so what?

SON: Then so what?

DAUGHTER: We shouldn't be afraid.

FATHER: Why did you come back?

SON: They tried to poison me out there in the snow.

DAUGHTER: Stay for dinner.

SON: Then what?

FATHER: You can't stay here.

SON: I'm staying.

DAUGHTER: He won't bite.

SON: I won't bite. I am not a wolf.

MOTHER: Where did you come from?

SON: Out there.

DAUGHTER: Out where?

FATHER: Out there, he said.

SON: I was born in 1835, and you know it.

FATHER: His mother's name was Molly.

SON: You are my mother.

FATHER: No.

MOTHER: She died in childbirth.

SON: And my father?

MOTHER: And the father had ridden off to get help.

FATHER: And was killed in a thunderstorm.

MOTHER: They thought that he'd been eaten by wolves.

FATHER: Then a girl over in San Felipe Springs reported seeing a creature and several wolves attacking a herd of goats.

MOTHER: The Apaches told stories of seeing children's footprints among wolf prints, so they organized a hunt.

FATHER: On the third day they cornered him in a canyon. The wolf mother with him was shot when she attacked the hunting party.

MOTHER: They tied him up and closed him up in a room.

FATHER: That night a large number of wolves attracted by his howling came to the ranch and stampeded the cattle, and he escaped.

MOTHER: He wasn't seen again for a year, until a surveying crew saw him on a sandbar near Devil River. He was with two pups. After that …

FATHER: They never saw him again. That's the story they tell.

MOTHER: Until we found him.

SON: That can't be true.

DAUGHTER: He is not a wolf.

FATHER: Wolf, vampire!

MOTHER: We took him, and he ran away, and now he's come back.

FATHER: To eat us.

DAUGHTER: No.

SON: You let me go.

FATHER: You ran away.

DAUGHTER: He did not run away.

MOTHER: Yes he did.

DAUGHTER: Mommy, no.

MOTHER: Mommy, yes.

FATHER: We found him on the sandbar and shot the pups.

MOTHER: Shall I tell you?

FATHER: He ran away.

MOTHER: Shall I tell you?

FATHER: We found him on the sandbar.

MOTHER: *(Reciting "The Vampire," by Buffy St. Marie.)*

Shall I tell you of the night? It was long ago.
Late November and the snow just about to fall.
And the moon was big and bright. Cold and sharp and clear.

And the air was biting.

Softly swiftly down the road. Never made a sound.

Someone came from far away. Someone tall and old.

As I looked into his eyes, no reflection came.

And I gave him bedding.

Oh, my little rosary, how I miss you so.

Never used you very well. Now I never will.

I am farther from you now than the two ends of eternity.

Now, I do his bidding.

DAUGHTER: He came on a horse, but no one was riding it.

MOTHER: And the air was biting.

FATHER: We found him on the sandbar.

MOTHER: No sandbar.

FATHER: Devil River.

SON: There is no Devil River.

DAUGHTER: Daddy.

MOTHER: It was a mistake.

SON: I am not a mistake.

FATHER: Wolf.

SON: I am not a wolf.

FATHER: Devil River.

SON: And I am not a wolf. You are my sister, but you are not a wolf.

Cut. Blackout. Music: Slowed chords from "She's a Woman," by The Beatles.

Son sits at table with rope around his neck. FATHER holds the end of rope and circles table. MOTHER sits at side chair with DAUGHTER's head in her lap.

MOTHER: Tell me something.

FATHER: What did you do for seven years out there on the wolf prairie?

SON: Nothing.

FATHER: What did you eat?

SON: Berries.

FATHER: You hung out with wolves.

SON: Yeah, so what?

MOTHER: Eating.

SON: Birds, rabbits, flowers, paper, flowers, tin cans—anything we could.

FATHER: Like a wolf.

SON: Paper.

DAUGHTER: Anything he could.

MOTHER: Paper?

DAUGHTER: So how long do you have to starve before you eat something else?

SON: I couldn't eat anything else.

DAUGHTER: There was nothing else.

SON: It got so cold, all the deer went away.

DAUGHTER: He had to eat anything.

SON: I tried to go to a farm. but they wouldn't let me in, they shot at me, scared me; so I went to a town, and the whole town was empty.

MOTHER: The iron ore gave out.

DAUGHTER: And you ate iron ore.

SON: I did. A rope from hell to hang him. I stayed by your cornfield till December. I ate cornstalks till they ran out. Then I killed a rabbit with my bare hands and I ate it. My tongue burned out from the blood.

FATHER: You loved the blood because you're a wolf.

MOTHER: Half-wolf.

SON: I hated the blood, but I had to eat it.

FATHER: You should have starved.

SON: But you eat rabbits.

FATHER: You should have starved.

SON: But you eat rabbits.

DAUGHTER: He had to eat.

SON: I ate my shoes, for God's sake.

DAUGHTER: I tried to find you by the cornfield, but you ran away. I went out there every day.

SON: And everyday I ran away. Then it got easier. Some people tried to catch me with ropes, so I bit them. But the wolves …

DAUGHTER: They were nice.

SON: They took me along.

FATHER: And you ripped up the sheep with them.

DAUGHTER: He had to.

FATHER: Leg of lamb.

SON: Yes sir.

FATHER: I wish you were a catfish.

SON: I wish I was too.

FATHER: But you're a wolf.

SON: I am not a wolf.

MOTHER: Half-wolf.

DAUGHTER: Half-boy.

SON: Damn right. But you ate the lambs.

FATHER: Damn right.

MOTHER: Something's burning.

DAUGHTER: The prairie's burning up.

MOTHER: If we lead it into a canyon, it'll burn itself out.

SON: It's getting near the town.

DAUGHTER: It's hitting the castanet factory. We could hear it exploding all night.

FATHER: You brought the fire.

SON: I started a fire in a cornfield to keep warm. It got very cold and chilly, and I started to worry.

DAUGHTER: And I called him to come here.

FATHER: And now he's catastrophizing everything.

DAUGHTER: He is not.

MOTHER: It's raining. The sun's coming out.

Cut. Blackout.

SON circles table with rope around his neck. FATHER sits on side chair and holds end of rope.

SON: If she is my sister, why isn't she a wolf?

MOTHER: Because of the man that came here one night.

FATHER: While I was gone.

SON: She is my sister and she is not a wolf, you are my mother and you are not a wolf, and you are my father and—

FATHER: I am not your father.

SON: But you eat sheep and rabbits, so—

DAUGHTER:—why aren't you a wolf?

FATHER: Go to sleep.

SON: She is my sister and she is not a wolf.

DAUGHTER: I am your sister, and then I am a wolf. So let's go out to the sea.

MOTHER: Don't go by the water.

DAUGHTER: We'll go to the water and be sea wolves.

SON: Then we can eat whatever we want.

DAUGHTER: We can eat paper if we want to.

SON: We can eat leaves if we have to.

DAUGHTER: Or birthday cakes if we want to. We'll go to the water because he's my brother, and I'm his sister, and—

SON:—we're wolves.

FATHER: You are not a wolf.

DAUGHTER: If he's a wolf, then I'm a wolf.

SON: I am not a wolf.

FATHER: Wolf, vampire, sleepwalker.

DAUGHTER: We'll go to the sea.

FATHER: Not into the water.

MOTHER: Sea wolves.

SON: And we'll eat fish and leaves and whales.

DAUGHTER: One time a man found two young pups on the beach and took them home to raise them. One day after they were grown the man saw them go out into the ocean and kill a whale. They brought the whale back to the shore so the man could eat it. Everyday it went like this. The wolves would go out and kill whales and bring back the meat. Soon there was so much meat lying around on the beach that it was going bad.

FATHER: When God saw this, He made a storm and brought down a fog, and soon the wolves could not find any whales to kill.

DAUGHTER: The waves were so high, the wolves could not even find their way back. They had to stay out there. Those wolves became sea wolves. Whale hunters.*

SON: We'll stay out there.

FATHER: You will not stay out there.

DAUGHTER: We'll stay out there.

MOTHER: You won't find your way back.

DAUGHTER: That's OK.

FATHER: Are you a wolf?

SON: *(Rising, pulling rope, and approaching FATHER. Speaking loudly.)* I am not a wolf. I told you, how many times do I have to tell you that I am not a wolf. They threw me out and I was living with the wolves for a few years and now I came back, but I am not a wolf. Understand? *Comprende?* Do I look like a wolf? No, so how could I be wolf, so I am not a wolf, all right? I am not a wolf vampire boy and I am not a wolf, all right? *(Whispering intensely into the face of FATHER.)* I am not a wolf. I told you, how many times do I have to tell you that I am not a wolf. They threw me out and I was living with the wolves for a few years and now I came back, but I am not a wolf. Understand? *Comprende?* Do I look like a wolf? No, so how could I be wolf, so I am not a wolf, all right? I am not a wolf vampire boy and I am not a wolf, all right?

MOTHER: Comprende.

SON: Dig it?

FATHER: I dig it.

SON: So get serious. *(Drops rope and begins circling table.)*

---

* Native American Northwest Coast story.

DAUGHTER: We'll stay out there.

MOTHER: You'll have to stay out there, and you won't find your way back.

DAUGHTER: That's OK.

SON: We'll stay out here.

DAUGHTER: I am your sister, and then I am a wolf, so let's go out to the sea.

SON: We'll stay here.

DAUGHTER: Then we are wolves, and we'll stay out there in the water. We'll stay out there.

MOTHER: You'll have to stay out there, and you won't find your way back.

DAUGHTER: That's OK.

SON: We'll stay out there.

DAUGHTER: I am your sister, and then I am a wolf, so let's go out to the sea.

SON: We'll stay there.

DAUGHTER: Then we are wolves, and we'll stay out there in the water.

Cut. Blackout. Music: "When I Saw You," by the Ronettes, skipping at "When, when …"

FATHER sits with SON's head on his lap.

SON: … and the snow was whitey white.

FATHER: When the sun sets, you'll be warm again. Tell me something.

SON: We'll go away and come back.

FATHER: How will you find you way back?

SON: We'll leave breadcrumbs all along the water.

FATHER: But the birds will eat them.

SON: The birds will eat them, but only the old birds will eat them and know it.

FATHER: The birds will eat them.

SON: The crumbs will have poison or sleeping pill in them, and the birds will eat them and die and leave their skeletons behind in a trail, and we'll follow the bones back, and the bones will sing, and we'll follow the song back as we hear it, and then we'll come back.

FATHER: You won't find your way back.

SON: Or else the birds will be asleep from the sleepy bread, but we'll wake them up as we follow them back and follow them back and follow them back, and then we'll be back, or maybe we'll never come back.

FATHER: If you go out there, you'll drown.

SON: If you follow us, you'll drown and, when you die, no one will come to your funeral.

FATHER: When I die and you bury me, I'll suck all the water from the ground, and you'll starve and die of thirst, and no one will come to bury you.

SON: I don't care.

FATHER: You'll become dead things floating in the water.

SON: I don't care.

Cut. Blackout.

Music: Ronettes' "When I Saw You," skipping interrupted by DAUGHTER screaming. All performers' eyes are heavily tearing during scene. DAUGHTER begins scene hysterically and ends deadpan. SON begins deadpan and ends hysterically. Actors often focus and move as if for a shifting imaginary camera.

DAUGHTER: *(Screaming.)* No I am not hysterical! I'm trying to tell you this as calmly as I know how. All right, Daddy. Yes, Daddy. Just now, not fifteen minutes ago. At the school. No I don't, just a minute. What's the name of the school, Mommy?

MOTHER: Just the Bodega Bay School.

DAUGHTER: The Bodega Bay School. Well I don't how many children—thirty or forty. No, the wolves didn't attack until the children were outside the school!

SON: Help you, Daddy?

FATHER: I need some change, Steve.

DAUGHTER: Wolves, I think. Oh I don't—Daddy, is there a difference between wolves and coyotes?!

FATHER: There is very definitely a difference, Miss.

DAUGHTER: Well they're different, Daddy! Well these were wolves, I think. Yes, hundreds of them. Yes, they attacked the children—attacked them. Well I don't know when, but I simply can't leave now, Daddy. All right, yes, goodbye!

FATHER: They're both perching wolves, of course, but quite different species. The wolf is called the Lupus and the coyote is Chapultepec.

DAUGHTER: Thank you. Do you have the number for the Faucett farm?!

MOTHER: Right here in this book, Valerie.

FATHER: I can't see that it makes any difference, wolves or coyotes. If the school was attacked, that's pretty serious.

MOTHER: I hardly think that either species would have sufficient intelligence to launch a mass attack. Their brain pans aren't big enough.

DAUGHTER: I just came from school, Mommy! I don't know anything about their brain pans, but—

SON: Well I do, I do know. Ornithology happens to be my avocation. Wolves are not aggressive creatures, Valerie. They bring beauty into the world. It is mankind …

MOTHER: Southern fried chicken and baked potatoes.

DAUGHTER: Yes, may I speak to Mr. Truffaut, please. Yes, I'll wait!

SON: It is mankind, rather, that insists on making it difficult for life to exist on this planet. Now if it were not for wolves …

FATHER: Steve, you don't seem to understand. Your sister said there was an attack on the school.

SON: Impossible.

DAUGHTER: Steve, I'm so glad I caught you. Something terrible has happened!

FATHER: It's the end of the world.

MOTHER: Bloody Marys.

SON: What actually happened at the school?

MOTHER: A bunch of wolves attacked the kids.

FATHER: It's the end of the world. "Thus said the Lord unto the mountains, and the hills, and the rivers, and the valleys. Behold, I, even I, should bring a sword upon you, and I will devastate your high places." Ezekiel, Chapter 16.

SON: "Woe unto them who rise up early in the morning that they may follow strong drink."

FATHER: Isaiah, Chapter 5. It's the end of the world.

SON: I hardly think a few wolves are going to bring about the end of the world.

DAUGHTER: These weren't a few wolves!

MOTHER: I didn't know there were many wolves in Bodega Bay this time of year.

SON: The wolf is a permanent resident throughout his range. In fact, during our Christmas count we recorded …

MOTHER: How many wolves did you count, Steve?

SON: Which wolves, Mommy? There are several varieties.

FATHER: The ones that have been playing devil with my fishing boats. That's when I knew.

DAUGHTER: Have you had trouble with wolves?

FATHER: One of my boats did last week. When I saw them, I knew I'd lose my mind.

MOTHER: This young lady was hit by a wolf only Saturday. We're frightening the children.

FATHER: A whole flock of wolves nearly capsized one of my boats. Practically tore the skipper's arm off.

SON: You're scaring the kids. Keep it low.

FATHER: Well you're scaring me. Are you trying to say that all these—ah, it sounds impossible.

MOTHER: I'm just telling you what happened to one of my boats.

SON: The wolves are after your fish, Mommy. Really, let's be logical about this.

DAUGHTER: What were the wolves after at the school?

SON: What do you think they were after?

DAUGHTER: I think they were after the children!

SON: For what purpose?!

DAUGHTER: To kill them!

SON: Why?!

DAUGHTER: I don't know why!

SON: For what purpose?!

DAUGHTER: To kill them!

SON: Why?!

DAUGHTER: I don't know why!

SON: I thought not. Wolves have been on this planet since archaeopteryx 140 million years ago. Doesn't it seem rather odd that they'd wait all that time to start a war against humanity?

DAUGHTER: No one called it a war.

SON: You and Daddy seem to be implying as much.

MOTHER: Who said anything about a war? All I said is some wolves—

DAUGHTER: Like some coffee?

MOTHER: No ... —came down on one of my boats. They could have been after the fish, just like you said.

FATHER: The captain should have shot them.

SON: Huh?!

FATHER: Wolves are scavengers anyway. Most Germans are. Get yourselves guns and wipe them off the face of the earth.

SON: That would hardly be possible!

MOTHER: Why not, Steve?

SON: Because there are 8,650 species of wolves in the world today, Mommy. It is estimated that five billion—

Music: Guitar chords from The Beatles' "Revolution," cut into Ronettes' "When I Saw You," skipping at "When, when ..."

FATHER: The wolves must have been after the Indians. Juke box doesn't work!

Music: Ronettes' song continues skipping—"...I ... when ... oh ..."—and ends with a deep scratching sound.

MOTHER: Stay way from that juke box!

SON: Maybe we're all getting a little carried away by this! Admittedly a few wolves did act strange, but that's no reason to believe—

DAUGHTER: I keep telling you this isn't a few wolves. These are foxes, coyotes, wolverines.

SON: I have never known wolves of different species to flock together! The very concept is unimaginable! Why, if that ever happened we ...

Cut. Blackout. Silence.

MOTHER: ... saw the attack at school. Why don't you believe her?

FATHER: What attack? Who attacked the school?

SON: Wolves did! You're all sitting here debating! What do you want them to do next, crash through that—

Blackout. Car skid. Music: Ronettes' "When I saw ..."

SON: As though nothing at all had happened! Poor things.

MOTHER: I'm leaving. Are you coming?

FATHER: It's the end of the world!

SON: Well I better get back to the cannery! Huh?!

MOTHER: I don't want to be an alarmist.

SON: No one ever said you were!

FATHER: No one ever said you were.

Music: Ronettes' "When I saw ..."

MOTHER: I think we're in real trouble.

FATHER: Stay way from that juke box!

SON: Huh?!

FATHER: I don't know how this started, or why; but I know it's here, and we'd be crazy to ignore it.

MOTHER: To ignore what, the wolf war?

FATHER: Yes, the wolf war. The wolf attack. Plague. Call it what you like. They're massing out there some place, and they'll be back. You can count on it.

MOTHER: Ridiculous.

SON: A one way ticket to hell!

MOTHER: Come here. Unless we do something right now.

SON: Look, Mom, even this is true, even if all—

MOTHER: Don't you believe it's true?

SON: No, Mom, frankly I don't. There's no reason!

MOTHER: Well it's happening. Isn't that a reason?

SON: Help how?! What do you want to do?!

Actors freeze during music: Ronettes' "Child, child, child ..."

MOTHER: Dad said something about Santa Cruz, about wolves getting lost in a fog and then flying towards the lights.

SON: We don't have any fog this time of year!

MOTHER: We'll make our own fog.

FATHER: How do you figure to do that?

MOTHER: We can use smoke pots, the way the army uses them.

DAUGHTER: *(Pointing, completely deadpan.)* Look they're attacking again.

SON: Now take it easy, Val. There isn't a wolf anywhere in sight!

FATHER: Look at the wolves of the air! They do not sow or reap, yet your heavenly Father feeds them!

MOTHER: Something like this happened in Santa Cruz last year. The town was just covered with wolves. Will you please finish your drink?

DAUGHTER: I recall it. A large flock of wolves got lost in a fog and headed into town where all the lights were.

FATHER: And they made some mess, too. Smashing into buildings and everything. They always make a mess.

DAUGHTER: The point is that no one seemed to be upset about it. They were all gone next morning, just as though nothing at all had happened, poor things.

FATHER: You brought them!

SON: I'm not a wolf!

MOTHER: I'm leaving. Are you coming?

Music: Ronettes' "When I saw you, / That's when I knew …"

FATHER: It's the end of the world!

SON: Well, I better get back to the cannery!

DAUGHTER: Steve, hold on a minute.

SON: Huh?!

DAUGHTER: I don't want to be an alarmist.

MOTHER: Your father said something about Santa Cruz, about wolves getting lost in a fog and then flying towards the lights.

SON: We don't have fog this time of the year!

MOTHER: We'll make our own fog.

FATHER: How do you figure that?!

MOTHER: We can use smoke pots the way the army uses them, you stupid motherfuckers!

DAUGHTER: Look! They're attacking again!

All look and point skyward in different directions.

FATHER: Look out!

DAUGHTER: Look at the gas. The man's lighting a cigar!

FATHER: Hey you! Don't drop that match! Get out of here!

MOTHER: Mister, run!

SON: Watch out!

DAUGHTER: Look out!

FATHER: Watch out!

Blackout. Music: Ronettes singing, "I'd lose my mind over you …"

MOTHER and DAUGHTER sit at the table facing each other.

MOTHER: How did you find your way back?

DAUGHTER: There was a big black rain, very thick, and he followed us, and we told him not to, and he followed us, and they both went down under a wave. They were swallowed up, and I waited and floated until the water threw me onto the dirt. And when I looked around, someone had blown all the bird bones away, and they weren't singing. Then the water threw me onto the dirt, and I could hear the sand walking behind me, and I looked around, and someone had plowed all the birds into the fields and dirt, but I could hear the bones singing underground faintly. Then the field turned black, and I ran back to the house.

MOTHER: Do you hear a knocking, a little knocking, a scratching?

DAUGHTER: No. They were drowned in a wave.

MOTHER: No.

DAUGHTER: They were Siamese fighting fish joined at the head, and they were drowned in a wave, and I came back.

MOTHER: No.

DAUGHTER: Yes. When I landed on the dirt, my eyes were all salty, erased. It was Tuesday.

MOTHER: No.

DAUGHTER: Yes.

Cut. Blackout.

Daughter: Just accept.

Mother: A coward never accepts, a coward never waits.

Daughter: Your son is dead.

Mother: My son is not dead and I am not a widow.

Daughter: My father is dead and my brother is dead.

Mother: My son is not dead and I am not a widow.

Daughter: I will be your son.

Mother: It's raining, the sun's coming out.

Daughter: I will be your son.

Mother: No.

Cut. Blackout.

Daughter: They were sold down the river and slaughtered.

Mother: Stop telling this. It sends my blood backwards.

Daughter: In the sea, where everything stays moist and rotten.

Mother: They'll come back.

Daughter: No.

Mother: We must wait.

Daughter: They're drowned.

Mother: We must be patient.

Daughter: How long shall we wait?

Mother: A while.

Daughter: How long?

Mother: Till this cigarette is finished.

Daughter: Twenty years.

MOTHER: Twenty years.

Cut. Blackout.

DAUGHTER: How long shall we wait?

MOTHER: As long as it takes. We must be patient.

DAUGHTER: They went under a wave forever.

MOTHER: You will wait by the beach everyday until the last tide comes in.

Blackout. Lights on. Silence.
Blackout. Cut.

DAUGHTER: I'm afraid you know that.

MOTHER: You're so pale and afraid.

DAUGHTER: I know.

MOTHER: As pale as a ghost pearl.

DAUGHTER: What do you have to lose?

MOTHER: Nothing. I've been dead several times already.

DAUGHTER: What is it really like?

MOTHER: It's not so bad. There's not much difference.

DAUGHTER: How could that be? But it can't be.

MOTHER: It can be. It will be.

DAUGHTER: What is there over there?

MOTHER: Nothing. Nothing at all.

DAUGHTER: Nothing at all. But that can't be.

MOTHER: You'll see.

DAUGHTER: No, I don't want to see.

MOTHER: It's not so bad. It's practically the same.

DAUGHTER: But it can't be. There isn't nothing on this side. It just can't be.

MOTHER: It's hard to tell.

DAUGHTER: How can you tell me there's nothing over here?

MOTHER: Because there is nothing. It's peaceful, soft; but as time goes by you climb.

DAUGHTER: Climb where?

MOTHER: Everywhere.

DAUGHTER: But why do you climb?

MOTHER: It's not really like climbing, it's just rising. You'll see.

DAUGHTER: Well, is it like smoke?

MOTHER: No. You're so pale.

DAUGHTER: I'm all right, I'm OK.

MOTHER: White water.

DAUGHTER: What are you trying to say? Don't try and take me with you.

MOTHER: I wouldn't do that. You'll go when—

DAUGHTER: When?

MOTHER: When your wheel of life turns to stone, a treadmill, a millstone, a crushed gland, a stained bitten apple, a kite with a cut string. When you can't fight the feeling anymore.

DAUGHTER: What feeling, when? What kite? You're trying to make me die.

MOTHER: No.

DAUGHTER: Well, is it like smoke?

MOTHER: No.

DAUGHTER: I can't fight the feeling anymore.

MOTHER: Yes you can.

DAUGHTER: I can't. Take me with you I can't fight it anymore.

MOTHER: Yes you can.

DAUGHTER: Is it like smoke?

MOTHER: No.

DAUGHTER: I can't.

MOTHER: Yes you can.

Cut. Blackout. Music: A slowed-down version of "She's A Woman," by The Beatles.

FATHER and DAUGHTER at table. She stares at him as he lip-synchs to the music. MOTHER sleeps at table.

Cut. Blackout. Music continues.

MOTHER and DAUGHTER sit at table looking at each other in silence.

Cut. Blackout. Music continues.

DAUGHTER: The house shook last night.

MOTHER: We must be patient.

DAUGHTER: Where will they come from?

MOTHER: The water.

DAUGHTER: How long?

MOTHER: Till there are no more tears left, till our eyes are erased, if we have to.

DAUGHTER: Tuesday to Tuesday I wait there every day till the last water comes in, and nothing. It goes over and over, rolls over and over like a roller coaster, rolls over and over.

MOTHER: No.

DAUGHTER: Yes.

Cut. Blackout. Music continues.

MOTHER: If we wait long and hard enough, they will come back.

DAUGHTER: Why?

MOTHER: We must be patient and try to sift it out.

DAUGHTER: Wait and wait and wait.

MOTHER: And wait. My patience is endless, petrified.

DAUGHTER: Like a singing dead bone.

MOTHER: We must be patient.

Cut. Blackout. Music continues.

MOTHER: Another few days.

Cut. Blackout. Music continues.

MOTHER: Have you come back?

SON: I've come back again.

MOTHER: Again and again.

DAUGHTER: Where are you?

SON: Washed to the other side of the salt sea.

DAUGHTER: For twenty tears.

SON: He's dead.

DAUGHTER: And buried under the water.

SON: What can I say?

MOTHER: Nothing.

DAUGHTER: Forever and ever.

MOTHER: The sea pulled him away.

SON: He was singing to me in a high clear voice, and the sea pulled him away. He's a drowned thing out there in the water.

DAUGHTER: And that's how it was.

SON: It was.

DAUGHTER: The cigarette is over.

MOTHER: Not yet. We must wait and see.

DAUGHTER: No more waiting.

Cut. Blackout. Music continues.

Lights up. BOY stands across stage from SON.

SON: Good morning.

MOTHER: How long has it been?

BOY: Seven years.

DAUGHTER: At least.

MOTHER: It's been a seven-year ache. We missed you.

BOY: You never missed me.

SON: You look so much like me.

BOY: I am you.

SON: You are not me.

BOY: I am you. That's why you can't look at me.

SON: I am not you.

MOTHER: He's not you.

DAUGHTER: Is he you?

SON: You hate me.

Boy: I love you even though you sent me away.

Son: You've got a strange kind of love.

Boy: Not strange.

Son: It's like burning.

Boy: Not burning.

Son: Strange.

Boy: Not so strange. I remember that vacation. *(Points arrow in Son's face, then breaks it in half and throws it to the floor.)*

Son: Don't talk about that vacation. Where did he come from?

Mother: Out there.

Son: Out where?

Daughter: I invented him in the water when I was swimming. Something in the water.

Son: Where is the father?

Daughter: Something in the water—a fish, a leaf—something.

Son: Where is the father?

Mother: We waited twenty years. We thought you had drowned.

Daughter: But you didn't.

Son: I have no son.

Boy: I'll be your son.

Daughter: One day I was by the water, and he floated in.

Mother: Like a dancing fish.

Son: Fish don't dance.

Mother: Yes they do.

Daughter: Then one day he swam away.

MOTHER: And now he's come back.

SON: Why have you come back?

BOY: I've come back again.

MOTHER: And again.

BOY: And again and again, until we get it right.

SON: How long are you staying?

BOY: I live in this house.

DAUGHTER: What does it matter?

SON: It matters because I become irked, disappointed, obliterated, it drags
    me—

DAUGHTER:—backwards.

BOY: I'm staying.

SON: No.

DAUGHTER: Just wait.

SON: I can't wait.

MOTHER: Then go drown again.

SON: He has to leave. *(He rises and begins circling the table in the opposite
    direction as the* BOY.*)*

DAUGHTER: Why?

MOTHER: He sends a pressure from down there.

SON: Where all the resources are.

DAUGHTER: When did he leave?

SON: He was four.

MOTHER: And now he's ten.

SON: We sent him away.

MOTHER: He ran away.

SON: He was killing everything.

MOTHER: The plants, the animals on the farm.

SON: He had to go.

MOTHER: So he ran away.

SON: And we said he died.

MOTHER: A vampire wolf boy.

SON: A wolf in his heart. What could we have done? He would have ended up amoral, violent, bestial, an animal machine.

DAUGHTER: Does he think he's a wolf?

MOTHER: Ask him.

BOY: I am not a wolf.

DAUGHTER: He is not a wolf.

SON: Wait until nightfall.

BOY: Daddy, I am not a wolf.

SON: Then where did the shark story come from?

BOY: Our vacation. I'm not a vampire wolf.

DAUGHTER: Or if you are, then so what?

BOY: Then so what?

DAUGHTER: We shouldn't be afraid.

SON: Why did you come back?

SON: They tried to poison me out there in the snow.

DAUGHTER: Stay for dinner.

BOY: The what?

SON: You can't stay here.

BOY: I'm staying.

DAUGHTER: He won't bite.

BOY: I won't bite. I am not a wolf.

MOTHER: Where did you come from?

BOY: Out there.

DAUGHTER: Out where?

SON: Out there, he said.

BOY: I was born in 1935, and you know it.

SON: His mother's name was Molly.

BOY: You are my mother.

SON: No.

MOTHER: She died in childbirth.

BOY: And my father?

MOTHER: The father had ridden off to get help.

SON: And was killed in a thunderstorm.

MOTHER: They thought he'd been eaten by wolves.

SON: Then a girl over in San Felipe Springs reported seeing a creature and several wolves, attack a herd of goats. (SON *throws* BOY *to the ground.*)

MOTHER: The Apaches told stories of seeing a child's footprints among wolf prints, so they organized a hunt.

SON: On the third day they cornered him in a canyon. The wolf mother with him was shot when it attacked the hunting party.

MOTHER: They tied him up and closed him up in a room.

SON: That night a large number of wolves, attracted by his howling, came to the ranch and stampeded the cattle, and he escaped.

MOTHER: He wasn't seen again for a year, until a surveying crew saw him on a sandbar near Devil River. He was with two pups. After that—

SON: They never saw him again.

MOTHER: That's the story they tell.

SON: Until we found him.

BOY: That can't be true.

DAUGHTER: He is not a wolf.

SON: Wolf, vampire.

MOTHER: We took him, and he ran away, and now he's come back.

SON: To eat us.

DAUGHTER: No.

BOY: You let me go.

SON: You ran away.

DAUGHTER: He did not run away.

MOTHER: Yes he did.

DAUGHTER: Mommy, no.

MOTHER: Mommy, yes.

SON: We found him on the sandbar.

MOTHER: No sand bar.

SON: Devil River.

BOY: There is no Devil River.

DAUGHTER: Daddy.

MOTHER: It was a mistake.

BOY: I am not a mistake.

SON: Wolf.

BOY: I am not a wolf.

SON: Devil River.

BOY: And I am not a wolf. You are my sister, but you are not a wolf.

Cut. Blackout. Music: Ronettes' skipping record—"When, when ..."

BOY lies with his head in SON's lap.

BOY: This story happened a very long time ago, when everything was very strange and cold. It just came out that way, there was no explanation, no reason, and that's how it was and it was. The sky tells them something. They had terrific hearts. The child was sleeping dark and deep and thick in the tender dead city where the iron ore had gave out. The city was quiet and dark and empty and tender and dead, and very sad and very empty. But there was a heart inside it somewhere still way down in a cavern, where all the iron had been dug out. But it was still in there, deep inside the mine. That's where it was, and it was there. Deep in there. The few birds left in the town went to look for it. They could tell it was there. So they went to look for it, and they flew in and down. But they got caught inside, and there wasn't any air to fly on or to breathe, so they died inside there with the heart, and the heart was so sad about this that it died soon after.

SON: Why do you tell me this sad story?

BOY: It's the saddest story I know.

Cut. Blackout. Previous music: The Beatles' "She's A Woman."

Boy and Mother dance in dim light with arrows to slowed/altered guitar break from "She's a Woman," The Beatles.

Cut. Blackout.

SON and BOY sit across from each other lengthwise at the table. MOTHER stands behind SON, and DAUGHTER stands behind BOY.

MOTHER: Tell me something.

SON: What did you do for seven years out there on the wolf prairie?

BOY: Nothing.

SON: What did you eat?

BOY: Berries.

SON: You hung out with wolves.

BOY: Yeah, so what?

MOTHER: Eating.

BOY: Birds, rabbits, paper, flowers, tin cans—anything we could.

SON: Like a wolf.

BOY: Paper.

DAUGHTER: Anything we could.

MOTHER: Paper?

DAUGHTER: So how long do you have to starve before you eat anything else?

BOY: I couldn't eat anything else.

DAUGHTER: There was nothing else.

BOY: It got so cold that all the deer went away.

DAUGHTER: He had to eat anything.

BOY: I tried to go to the farm, but they wouldn't let me in. They shot at me, scared me; so I went to a town, and the whole town was empty.

MOTHER: The iron ore gave out.

DAUGHTER: And you ate iron ore.

BOY: I did. A rope from hell to hang him. I stayed by your cornfield till December. I ate cornstalks till they ran out. Then I killed a rabbit with my bare hands, and I ate it. My tongue burned out from the blood.

SON: You loved the blood because you're a wolf.

MOTHER: Half-wolf.

BOY: I hated the blood, but had to eat it.

SON: You should have starved.

BOY: But you eat rabbits.

SON: You should have starved.

BOY: But you eat rabbits.

DAUGHTER: He had to eat.

BOY: I ate my shoes, for God's sake.

DAUGHTER: I tried to go out and find you by the cornfield, but you ran away. I went there every day.

BOY: And every day I ran away. Then it got easier. Some people tried to catch me with ropes, so I bit them. And the wolves ...

DAUGHTER: They were nice.

BOY: They took me along.

SON: And you ripped up the sheep with them.

DAUGHTER: He had to.

SON: Leg of lamb.

BOY: Yes sir.

SON: I wish you were a catfish.

BOY: I wish I was, too.

SON: But you're a wolf.

BOY: I am not a wolf.

MOTHER: Half-wolf.

DAUGHTER: Half-boy.

Boy: Damn right. But you ate the lambs.

Son: Damn right.

Mother: Something's burning.

Daughter: The prairie's burning up.

Mother: If we lead it into a canyon it'll burn itself out.

Boy: It's getting near the town.

Daughter: It's hitting the castanet factory. We could hear it exploding all night.

Son: You brought the fire.

Boy: I started a fire in a cornfield to keep warm. It got very cold and chilly, and I started to worry.

Daughter: And I called him here.

Son: And now he's catastrophizing everything.

Daughter: He is not.

Mother: It's raining, the sun's coming out.

Son: Are you a wolf?

Boy: (*Jumps on table top and crouches in front of Son. Loudly.*) I am not a wolf. I told you, how many times do I have to tell you that I am not a wolf. They threw me out and I was living with the wolves for a few years and now I came back, but I am not a wolf. Understand? *Comprende?* Do I look like a wolf? No, so how could I be wolf, so I am not a wolf, all right? I am not a wolf vampire boy and I am not a wolf, all right? (Boy *jumps off table, his face close to the* Son's.)

Son and Boy: (*Staring into each other's eyes.*) I am not a wolf. I told you, how many times do I have to tell you that I am not a wolf. They threw me out and I was living with the wolves for a few years and now I came back, but I am not a wolf. Understand? *Comprende?* Do I look like a wolf. No, so how could I be wolf, so I am not a wolf, all right? I am not a wolf vampire boy and I am not a wolf, all right?

MOTHER: *Comprende.*

BOY: Dig it?

SON: I dig it.

BOY: So get serious.

SON: We don't have any fog this time of year.

MOTHER: We'll make our own fog.

SON: How do you figure to do that?

BOY: We can use smoke pots the way the army uses them, you stupid motherfuckers!

DAUGHTER: Look, they're attacking again!

BOY: Look out!

DAUGHTER: Look at the gas. That man's lighting a cigar.

SON: Hey you, don't drop that match! Get out of there!

MOTHER: Mister, run!

SON: Watch out!

DAUGHTER: Look out!

BOY: Watch out!

Cut. Blackout. Music: Ronettes' song skipping at "When, when …"

MOTHER and FATHER sit in chairs on either side of the stage facing each other. SON and DAUGHTER lie on backs on center table with heads hanging over edge and facing audience.

MOTHER: It's the steady beat that keeps you amused.

FATHER: It seems to be so.

MOTHER: It seems to be so.

FATHER: To the child, you're a child.

SON: I seem to be. I guess I am, aren't I?

DAUGHTER: Hit the road, shithead.

MOTHER: If you two do not be quiet I am going to get so mad.

SON: We're sorry …

FATHER: You have been talking all night.

MOTHER: Please calm down.

FATHER: Settle down.

MOTHER: And go to sleep.

DAUGHTER: Now you've gotten crumbs all in the bed.

FATHER: What?

SON: Nothing.

MOTHER: What?

DAUGHTER: Nothing. We're going to sleep now, sorry.

FATHER: I don't want another peep out of you.

MOTHER: Not another peep.

FATHER: What?

SON: Not another peep. We're becoming rock formations, dead to the world.

MOTHER: What about rock formations?

DAUGHTER: Dead to the world. Goodnight.

FATHER: Goodnight.

SON: Grand Canyon.

MOTHER: What?

DAUGHTER: Bless Grandfather.

FATHER: Goodnight.

SON: Voodoo. Do you believe in it?

MOTHER: Will you quiet down.

DAUGHTER: Silence . . .

SON: Rock formations. Open the window.

FATHER: Be quiet.

DAUGHTER: No, tiptoe.

SON: Too much. It's windy downstairs.

MOTHER: Did you open a window up there?

DAUGHTER: Rock formations.

FATHER: Now be quiet.

MOTHER: Sleepwalkers.

FATHER: Time goes too slowly. All those flutes make me so nervous like a mouse under water.

DAUGHTER: He tapped the lampshade and dust came out of it.

FATHER: It was human or was once human. It was frightening.

SON: Did it have a ghost?

FATHER: I however prefer to be interrupted by life now and then.

MOTHER: From time to time.

FATHER: What is the name of that raw living shellfish one eats in the south of Italy? It crawls down your throat alive and then of course dies.

MOTHER: I don't know.

FATHER: Ever heard of it?

MOTHER: Never did.

FATHER: Ever do it?

MOTHER: Never did.

FATHER: Don't know.

MOTHER: Never did ever do it.

FATHER: Never did.

MOTHER: Never heard of it.

DAUGHTER: Quiet down there.

SON: Yeah we're trying to get some sleep.

FATHER: You're going on a journey.

MOTHER: Your journey continues.

SON: Where?

FATHER: Everywhere.

MOTHER: You are a flying rock formation flying through the air.

FATHER: You're a rock but you can feel the air.

DAUGHTER: I'm a rock but I can feel the air.

SON: Make my bed soon, I'm sick to the heart and I'll faint. What'll I do?

MOTHER: You're faint. A fainting rock.

SON: But I am not a wolf.

FATHER: You are not.

DAUGHTER: And I am not a wolf.

SON: And she is my sister but I am not a wolf.

FATHER: You're asleep but you are flying and you are not a wolf.

SON: Grand Canyon.

DAUGHTER: Rock formations. We'll stay out there.

MOTHER: You'll have to stay out there and you won't find your way back.

DAUGHTER: That's OK.

SON: We'll stay out there.

DAUGHTER: I am your sister and then I am not a wolf so let's go out to the sea.

SON: We'll stay there.

DAUGHTER: Then we are wolves and we'll stay out there in the water.

FATHER: You are asleep but you are flying and you are not a wolf.

MOTHER: You are a rock but you can feel the air.

SON: I am a rock but I can feel the air.

DAUGHTER: Ditto.

MOTHER: OK?

DAUGHTER: OK.

FATHER: OK?

SON: OK.

MOTHER/FATHER: OK?

DAUGHTER/SON: OK.

Slight Return

For Ethyl Eichelberger

Slight Return was first performed in a co-production with La MaMa E.T.C. and Randolph St. Gallery at Randolph St. Gallery, Chicago, November 1994.

Cast

K: Kyle Decamp
VOICES:

     S: Sanghi Wagner
     J: Jessica Liebman
     B: Black-Eyed Susan
     F: Michael Tighe
     D: David Cale
     1: Mario Oliver
     2: Alejandro Reyes
     3: Arturo Reyes
     4: Martín Acosta

CLAUDIA, F, and J voices are heard simultaneously

Mike Taylor, *Technical Director and Lighting Design*

Directed and designed by John Jesurun

A 7-by-7-foot room sits on the stage. The actor performs the entire piece concealed inside this closed room. Five live cameras are set in the walls of this room. The audience sees the action inside the room on five 3-by-4-foot projection screens hung side-by-side in front of the room.

Lines marked K are spoken live by the performer. All other voices are on audiotape.

S, B, and J are female voices. F and D are male voices.

1, 2, 3, and 4 are male voices with Mexican accents.

1. Who Said That?

K: Who said that?

S: Is anyone there?

K: Where are you?

S: Where are you?

K: Who are you? It's too dark in here. I can't see a thing … It's too dark in here, I can't see a thing, I said.

S: Can't you manage to turn on a light?

K: Who said that?

S: I think there's a switch in there.

K: Well, I don't see a fucking thing.

S: Look around. Feel around on the walls. I think there's a switch.

K: No, there isn't.

S: Isn't there a TV in there?

K: On one channel there's *Hitler's Daughter,* and on the other, there's *The Diary of Anne Frank.* They've been playing continuously for two months, and I'm fucking sick of it!

S: Don't they have anything else?

K: No! And quit playing that sad guitar; it's giving me a nauseosis. There's something burning in here!

S: There's a fire in there!

K: There's a toilet in here! What is this place? And turn off that air conditioning!

S: Get back to where you once belonged.

F: Where's that?

K: You tell me. Where is that fucking light switch?

Faint music: "Run Away," by Bronski Beat.

K: Bronski, is that you?

F: No.

K: Shit, no! There's someone else in here, I know it, I can hear them breathing. A heart beating, someone … tiny, a tiny person, or something!

S: A fly?

F: Hardly! What room are you in?

K: How the hell would I know? Where is that switch? … Jesus, this is such a magical misery tour! Don't turn on the lights! I just realized I must be naked. Let me at least put on my underwear, if I can find it.

S: I can't turn on the lights.

K: I know I was wearing my underwear when I fell asleep.

F: Find it?

K: No. Am I the walrus? I said, am I the walrus?!

S: I don't think so. What room did you say you were in?

K: Is there any soap around? I have to take a bath.

S: Who said that?

F: It's me.

K: Who are you?

S: Don't ask him, he doesn't know anything.

K: Four thousand holes in Blackburn, Lancashire, and this certainly is one. Hello? Hey! Where are you? Great! Now he left, the jerk.

F: Probably smoking pot somewhere.

K: Oh, you shut up! Would you please call the main office and have me removed from here immediately?

S: You're awfully far down, and the surrounding area is devastated, as you may know!

K: No, I may not know.

F: What room are you in? I'll call you back.

K: Don't hang up! Don't ha—

This is what people do to each other. This is what people do for each other. This is what people do for themselves when they can't do for themselves. Where is that switch? Do you see the sparkle? The sparkle is from tons of silver-iron ore in the air. It fell from the sky for days. I suppose a silver-iron mine exploded in the earthquake, but it's stopped now. This is a letter that blew in on a hot wind one day when I was on the roof. It floated over from the direction of the volcano known as Number Six. I had it mailed two weeks before, and now the fucking thing comes back to me. The letters on the page are dead, abdicated. The debris field is magnificent. Oh, well ... the Lord has loosed a mighty sword on the dwarf planet.

F: Are you there? Is you there?

K: I'm cold.

S: You're sparkling!

K: I know. I've got to wash my face. It's covered in silver ore. *Mi casa definitely no es su casa.*

Sound of rain. A video image of a cat inside the room appears briefly.

2. Story to Cat

K: Now, honey, I don't know any more stories … Yes, I do. No, I don't know what happened to the leader of the country or the government here. After the earthquake I suppose that eventually the humiliated leader burnt or buried his treasures and left for the Gulf Coast. Now, there are at least two stories of what he did when he got there. Would you like to hear them? Good. One is that he put on a turquoise mask and feather headdress and set himself on fire and became the morning star. The other is that he set sail eastward and promised to return someday. Which one?

Shall I then burn and bury my treasures, my silver face? Anyway, after he left, they slaughtered the town and rebuilt it in their own fashion. The rest of the inhabitants died of grief, and it became a reconstructed city, but an empty one. A city of God, a heavy thing, a very heavy thing. I never doubted its beauty, even reconstructed … or, perhaps I did. The ghastly beauty of those clear, watery, dying eyes.

S: I never doubted their beauty. It's raining again. I'm not dead. I'm only sleeping.

3. A Long Time Already

K: But I've known that for a long time already. It's cold in here, and I can't see anything. Where's that flashlight? "When you're lost in Juarez in the rain and it's Easter time, too."

F: And what were your conclusions?

K: Who knows?! I had some soup. There were police sirens all night all over the city during the earth palpitations, or whatever. I couldn't sleep.

F: What became of your assistant, Mrs. Peabody?

K: Was she American?

F: Yes.

K: Then she was dead before she got here. And in case you were wondering what happened to me, when the mountain blew its lid, the guns started. The building started to shake like a jukebox, and everyone left the hotel; so I cleaned up a bit. And it was a mess, a brick shithouse. Then Abe said, "Where you want this killing done? Out on highway sixty one." And they did, and they ran away. And the headless mountain said, "After the slaughtering of the hogs, take everything down to the highway and dump it, hump it!" And they did. My complexion has deteriorated.

The ones who weren't dumped were humped, turned into whores. Well, I almost did, too. I heard myself scream, "Somebody help me!" And nobody did, because there was no one there. "Somebody, please, help me!" And something did. In the middle of a violent hailstorm: the cat. The cat I found chewing on a skeleton. Mr. Peabody, I think. Mr. XX, I presume? The cat nodded yes. Oh, by the way, Cinderella was also killed, but of course raped first by her own ugly sisters with the glass slipper that fit her so well. They took it off her tiny foot, smacked her once in the forehead, and that was it. The stars hid their faces in shame. If the shoe fits, wear it. *(Sings.)* "Fly away, Linda Paloma ... " It's cold in here. They dumped her with an old scarecrow and her dear old friend Ophelia, who had expired earlier. Under a filthy, scuzzy, disgusted rainbow. It was frightful! Then a wall collapsed and buried them all together. The cat whispered in my ear, "Don't worry, magic is everywhere around you."

F: And you? What happened to you?

K: Nothing. I stayed behind a tree, where I was hiding. I hid there for a week or so. The cat and I caught an empty locomotive West, anywhere, to the Coast, where we got lost among a tribe of leper Indians who didn't know where they were either.

F: What a trip. What a weird, wild ride.

K: Not so weird, really. I poisoned all their religious texts to punish them for tearing out the cat's tongue in a treacherous, messy ceremony. And they licked the blood and they liked it! Oh yes, they liked it. Then all the widows of the village leapt into the sea. Their children followed them. Every child returns to the flowery smell of its mother. Praised be the widows of the universe all across the universe. Now blossoms grow in their breasts, and mermaids eat them. Well, after that display we couldn't stay there, so the cat and I walked all the way back along the highway. Yes, the infamous Highway 61.

Sound: Hendrix guitar.

4. We Fell Asleep

K: We fell asleep in a house by a lagoon. At sunrise everything moved again. But, as I remember, I woke up covered with white dust, or mud, or something. The lagoon was filled with the houses that once surrounded it. The house I fell asleep in was gone. My transistor radio was on my chest playing a song by George Michael. I looked at it, and it stopped. Thank God. I can't stand that song. Anyway, after the earthquake I made my way up to a luxury hotel I noticed once on the main strip. It was empty. And of course, all the Americans in it were dead, way dead. I walked right past the bloody lobby and took the elevator to the twelfth floor swimming pool, which was full of pink water. I found an empty suite and installed myself. The air conditioning still worked. I tried room service, but no one answered. They were probably all dead down there in the kitchen among the rotting tamales and putrid, putrefying guacamole. Animal, vegetable, and mineral rotting together. So I went down to see if I could scrounge a meal. And yes, I was right. Flies covered everything; but I did manage to get some ice cream out of a freezer. I covered my head with a bandana to keep away the smell. The cat carried a chrysanthemum to keep away the flies. Rocky Road: 120 gallons. It lasted me a long time. Who could ask for anything more? I drained the pool because it was covering over with blood-sucking algae. We peeked over the edge of the rooftop patio and saw the entire pool contents drain into the empty street. Now I can sleep at night in the empty pool.

J: When are you leaving?

K: I don't know. When the ice cream runs out.

J: When will that be?

K: Soon, I suppose. I keep looking out over the city, but I don't see any movement. Once in a while a plane goes over.

J: Why?

K: They go west, always to the west. The city is dead. It was already dead when I arrived. The people I met were just ghosts living a prematurely retroactive life. That's why they all lied so much. Ghosts always lie.

Hendrix music.

5. One Hot Second

K: I became hysterical, but just for one hot second, when I came upon a skull in a garbage can while chasing a fly. The cat threw it over the side of the hotel, and we watched its tear-stained cheeks shatter in the alleyway below. Whammo! Bango! Bull's-eye! It echoed all over the city and etched itself into the street.

J: How do you like that?

K: I don't.

J: What else?

K: Have you done anything about getting me out of here yet?

J: We're trying.

K: Trying what?

J: What else?

K: Then it rained again. Did I mention I had a baby during that time?

J: No! Where is it?

K: I don't know. I left it by the pool one day after feeding it ice cream, and it disappeared. I searched the street below to see if it had fallen, but I couldn't find a trace. I wait for its return someday. I hope it will return someday. I'll have to stay here until it returns to the flowery smell of its mother. I didn't know I was pregnant at all, I don't think.

J: Oh dear.

K: I keep calling room service, but no one answers, all right?!

J: Okay.

K: I began to think that who I am is the wrong person. I'm the wrong person in this body. What do I look like? Can you see me? And if I'm the wrong person, then who aren't I?

6. Maybe Baby

K: Am I getting older, or younger?

D: Is the sun going up, or down?

K: Oh! I hear something in the street. Maybe it's my baby.

D: What is it?

K: Nothing. A flock of birds hording around a dead dog. There are so many here. I keep hearing someone playing guitar at night in the hotel. I think someone is alive in the hotel—someone else. I called every funky, fucking number of every room in the hotel, and no one answers. So I go down at night to follow the sound, but I can't locate it. It changes location. Every night it's in a different room. Then one night it stopped, and I didn't hear it again for weeks. Then it started again.

Music: Strains of "Don't Leave Me This Way," by Thelma Houston, triple-tracked.

K: Hear it?

D: No.

K: Well, I do. It's right below me now.

D: What kind of guitar?

K: Electric. A stratocaster 211.

D: What kind of music—Mexicana, folk, or rock?

K: Where is my baby?

D: Maybe the baby is playing the guitar.

K: The guitar is bigger than he is!

D: Is it a boy?

K: Yes, as far as I could tell. I called room service one night, and someone answered.

D: Shit! What did they say?

K: Nothing. I said, "Hello?" and they hung up.

D: Maybe it's the baby.

S: Your power is running low. Your screen has dimmed.

K: So what the fuck do you expect me to do? You want me to ask the cat to fix it? Then I hear a baby crying.

D: Perhaps it's returned slightly.

K: Then one night my phone rang. For a while I was too scared to keep calling different phone numbers.

S: Did you call the police?

K: The police? They're dead every everywhere! And thank God! They were pigs anyway.

D: The Red Cross?

K: There is no Red Cross here.

S: Where are you now?

K: Hell if I know! If you can see me, why can't you tell me where I am?

D: Not enough information.

K: What more information do you need? What do I look like? What color hair do I have? How tall am I?

S: Taller than the cat.

K: Am I wearing shoes?

D: No shoes.

K: I'm feeling sick. *(Vomits.)*

S: Keep talking. What happened when the phone rang? Did you pick it up?

D: Did you pick it up?

K: Did you pick it up!

D: Don't sass back!

K: I'm feeling sick, I said!

S: Did you pick it up?

K: No. It rang all night, so I let it ring. The cat and I went up to the pool and slept in there. We could hear the phone ringing all night, the only sound in the city, this fucking dead city!

D: Did it ring again?

K: It rang again every night for months. I couldn't sleep for weeks. Who needs sleep, anyway, in a dead city?

S: What about sex?

K: Well, I've always been able to take care of myself when I have to.

D: Oh, what a bore!

K: Yes, indeed. And the cat has lots of friends in the alleyway. Sometimes it gets stoned. There's tons of grass in the hotel safe from the tourists, and a lot of money. But what good is that, if you can't buy anything? I counted it: a million dollars in their weird currency that is now worth NOTHING! *(Throws money into the air.)* But it wasn't worth anything to begin with.

S: And the people?

K: People? What people? I told you they were all dead! And the people! They were dead before they were dead. The people! They were hardly people. A wretched race of lying, stealing, conniving, strangulated minions. I grew to hate them, despite all the flowers. They were half-dead, and now they're all dead. The country is totally fucked! Absolutely illegal tender!

D: Back to the phone.

K: I finally picked it up; but it spoke in a language I didn't understand, and I could hear a baby crying.

S: What room are you in? Where are you?

K: In another hotel across the city to see if we can get some more ice cream. We're running out. It took us a week to get across the city. We kept losing our way. That cat has no sense of direction, and the map was no good. Blocks had been obliterated, and there were no streets. When I finally got there, the hotel was locked; but there were lights on inside.

B: Was there a baby there?

K: Was there a baby there? Who's that? Do I know you?

B: It's me.

K: Then I noticed my hair had all turned gray. Then I noticed there was some movement across the city, and people were beginning to return, and I had to move on. Who knows what they would do to me, or why or who they even were? What would they do to a gray-haired woman with no baby, a cat, and two tons of Rocky Road. And it was a rocky road. Lights began to appear in the city, where previously there were none. We ran back to the hotel.

B: Which hotel?

K: The first hotel, formerly the Casa Blanca, which I now call La Casa Negra, the Black House, because it's covered in ash from all the psychic eruptions of its former inhabitants. I never doubted its ugliness, but I've changed. I turned out all the lights in the hotel, so they wouldn't think I was there.

B: Didn't you want them to find you?

K: No. Then I began hearing something on the TV. I saw that people began to stream in from the country next door.

B: What country?

K: I don't know, the one next door. The language, all the pictures were of places I'd never seen.

B: What did the people look like?

K: Different, all different colors. No way to tell who they were or what they were saying.

B: Your hair isn't gray; it's all white!

K: My beautiful hair! Am I some kind of old woman?

B: Who knows?

D: No big deal.

K: Look! Maybe we should all just shut up for a minute, all right? Somewhere along the way we were led astray into an ashtray, where we burnt out. Or, how I was involved?

B: Or was I involved at all?

D: Or was I?

K: Or am I?

B: Well, I'm not.

K: I don't know. When I woke up I was naked. I had a diet coke, and I had been listening to a Beatles record when the first pre-shock came. Are you there?

D: Yes.

B: Stop crying.

K: Look, lover boy, when I cry, everyone cries.

D: Okay.

K: Anyway, it was seven o'clock.

B: In the morning?

K: Stop interrupting me!

D: Sorry.

K: Hold on tight! Here comes another shock!

Explosion sounds. Flashes of light on screens.

K: What's going on out there? Anyway, I think the city was just waking up, except it never woke up; but I did. I got a call from the front desk saying to run away. Where to? I said. I heard a scream, and they hung up. And I didn't run away. Everyone else did, or they were killed. Well, the Americans didn't run; but they don't run away from anything, they run into it.

B: Not always a good idea. *(B and D laugh.)*

K: Oh, ha ha! I went up to the pool for a swim; but as I said, it was all pink. It was raining all over the place. It must have been spring, because the heavy rains came. Dark, insatiable rains. Excuse me, I have to eat now. Do you mind?

D: She's in there, but not really.

B: Hush up.

D: Well, tell her to put something on, for God's sake!

K: What do you mean? I'm not naked, am I? Are you sure you can't see me?

B: We can only hear you.

K: Well, I can only hear myself, too. Anyway, that's when it happened. After I found the cat. Soon after the third eruption. The third day after we returned to the hotel, I began getting phone calls again. This time the phone was breathing. I found the source was on the seventh floor.

D: What did you find?

K: A naked body. And, of course, I had to kill it.

B: What do you mean?

K: A beam had fallen on her, and she was a mess, cut in half. He had blue eyes.

D: Who?

K: She said her name was Claudia. He must have been lying there for weeks, trying to call me. She was naked, white, a hermaphrodite. He said, "Kill me. Please, kill me." And so I had to do it. I killed him because she was dying. "Please, kill me." Those were the last human words I heard for months. I killed him with a seductive five-inch stiletto I found in the closet. I remember the sweat on your brow dripping. God speed your love to me, so I did it. Poor Claudia, your broken, brittle tongue, your glass lips shattered. God speed your love to me, and I did it. I did it! My little heart was beating fast. The cat whispered in her ear, "Don't fear, magic is everywhere around you," and I did it! This place is totally fucked! You send me to look at this fucking volcano, and now I'm trapped in here, and I can't get out! An eleven-story morgue, a necropolis, a city of un-God. Living the life of a necrophiliac because you can't get it together to send a fucking helicopter to airlift me out! I'll have to sit here and wait for the authorities, who will of course accuse me of killing everyone in the hotel. I'll admit at times I wanted to, but I didn't.

But nature has a way of flushing itself out like a volcano. And the only person I killed I didn't want to. And after all those phone calls. Oh! I'm having a great time!

B: We're trying to help you.

K: Help me? You're trying to fucking kill me!

D: Do you have any message you want to send back?

K: Oh, thank you very much.

B: Do you?

K: Yes. Bunny Lake is missing! Anyway, I filled the room with flowers and sealed it. It's room 754, if you want to know. Now, if you don't mind, I'm going to wash myself off. *(K washes off slowly with water and sponge.)* Just thinking about that story makes me feel filthy. So turn around. I said, turn around! I know you're looking at me ... Oh, I don't care. And now, if you will excuse me, I'm going to sleep, and don't try to follow me! Goodnight. *(Screens dark.)* Don't bother sitting there. I'm going to sleep. I'll see you in the morning, whenever that is, which I suppose is whenever I wake up. So sign off! And, for your information, the cat is going to sleep, too. Aren't you, honey? And when we wake up, we will rock you!

Music. Guitar break from "We Will Rock You," by Queen. Rain.

7. 2,000 Years

F: Where are you?

K: We've disappeared for a while. I feel like I've been in here for two thousand years.

F: What are you doing in there?

B: Sleeping?

K: I'm not sleeping. I'm dead.

F: Okay, be that way.

B: Another one bites the dust.

K: Look, I'm leaving the light off! If I can't see you, then you won't see me.

F: Even-steven.

K: Who are you?

B: No one.

K: Then shut up and let's keep it that way! Someone was in here last night.

F: Really?

K: It was one of you.

B: Impossible!

K: Someone came in here last night, I heard them. They came in and leaned over the bed. I could feel their breath on my eyelids. I could feel it! It was you, wasn't it?

F: Impossible!

K: I could feel a man's breath on my face.

B: How could you be sure it was a man?

K: It was a man's hard breath, and a cold piece of steel touched my shoulder.

F: Maybe it was the cat.

K: No.

B: Perhaps it was the hermaphrodite.

K: She's dead! I told you I killed him! Someone was in here, breathing over me.

F: It was your guardian angel.

K: Guardian angel?! If he's my guardian angel, why was he holding a gun?

B: He's guarding you.

K: From what? From getting me out of this freaking Andalusian hellhole! And his breath stunk like pigshit! It had to be you! Jim! Are you there?

F: Yes.

K: When is that helicopter arriving?

B: We just don't know.

K: I could feel your breath on my lip. It had all the delicacy of a refried bean. It was you!

B: Are you there?

K: It was you!

F: Are you there? Are you there?

Music: "Don't Leave Me This Way." Rain.

8. Dialogue of the Hermaphrodite

K: Before I killed her, we had lunch. How long have you been here? Claudia? Claudia? Are you there?

CLAUDIA: *(Languid voices of a man and woman speaking simultaneously.)* I came to the Casa Negra rather late in time, before the heavy rains. Since I was arriving by helicopter, my first view was of the roof. Below me I could see the maid, Chinita, and the waitress, Penthesilea, eating sandwiches. The lustrous little army! I was happy then. Who the hell knows why, but they knew why. Where were you? I didn't see you. Yeah, well, they had a little radio, and they were listening to French pop songs. They led me down the stairs. A row of vestal virgins guarding what was to become your fortress of solitude. A blackened crater turned inside-out. Before it turned outside-in and in upon itself. "Thank you for inviting me. I've been looking forward to this all year," said Chinita. We entered the crater. It was unparalleled in its magnificence. It had become enclosed by itself, within itself. Who was it that warned me not to go near the Casa Negra? What happened, you ask? Exploding confusion and desecration, taking it apart stone by stone by grain of cement into powder transmogrified—so help me God, it could happen to you. How many times have I been through this before? The elevator technician was hanging from the balcony, bared and naked, pieces of fingers flying in five directions, a greasy grease monkey. The first second of the first convulsion. And the sound? It ran into the moon and exploded, howling like a broken guitar. Flying in the face of living air, five tones and four points hitting at regular intervals caressed me tightly against the walls. And the space? The place? The taste? Walls swaying, pisspot, coriander, artemis, jackpot. It needed nothing to propel it. "Nothing?" you ask. Not nothing. A box of light, a surprise, at last, in the end, finally.

K: Sandwich?

Claudia: Thanks. And me? A broken nose, bleeding without a face, flying in the face of dead air. Thus spoke the headless mountain mouth in a gust of methane breath. Thus spoke Krakatoa, Haleakala, Penthesilea, Taormina.

K: Where are you?

Claudia: I'm on the threshold of rapture, and you're the one. You are the one I've been waiting for so long, the one I've been dreaming of. You are the one I've been waiting for, the one I've been dreaming of. Don't be afraid.

You are the one I've been dreaming of. Push me over the edge. I'd do it for you. You are the one I've been waiting for. I've been waiting for you. Take away my sense of gravity. I've been waiting. Take away my gravity. Come on down and do what you've got to do. I'd do it for you. You are the one. I've waited a lifetime for this second and this second only, this one second. Give me this one second, and then take it away from me. Send me forward. "Don't leave me this way. I can't survive. I can't stay alive without your love. Don't leave me this way. I can't exist. I'll surely miss your tender kiss. Don't leave me this way." Give me this one second, and then take it away. Satisfy the need in me, and then take it away.

Kill me, please. Please, kill me, and let me live again. Satisfy the need in me. Don't leave me this way. Don't be afraid; there is magic everywhere around me. Don't leave me this way.

Music: Triple-tracked "Don't Leave Me This Way." Rain sounds.

9. Tincture

K: The sun came out of everywhere and burned everything dry. It hasn't rained in weeks. It stayed in the same corner of the sky for weeks.

J: Isn't it fascinating?

K: I refuse to be fascinated. Since then I've been covered with this kind of … tincture. It comes out of my skin, but I don't know. I must inhale it in the air, and then it later is released from an area below my skin. It's a tincture. The texture of merthiolate—the same hue and texture, more watery than water, deeper then grenadine, but on the skin a tone of yellow, saffron, orange, tangerine, tamarind. When is that helicopter coming? You know, it's impossible to breathe in here. There's enough air, but it's thin air or something. I get light-headed and headachy. Every once in a while I have to inhale a huge breath to keep my lungs filled up. What is that? What kind of air? I wonder if it has anything to do with the whatever it is that later appears on my skin. My skin! My poor skin. It was so fresh once. Now it feels so … greasy, almost, from that tincture.

J: Well, anyway, don't let it bother you. You'll be out of there soon enough.

K: The city is covered with dead butterflies that fell out of the sky. It left a stream of butterfly blood across the sky, across my universe. It must be some kind of butterfly blood. The fluid in it evaporates on contact with the air, leaving this faint, saffron-color stain and the smell of rotting guava. Still there? Steve? Steve? Still there? No? Okay. Then I became cold and afraid. My delicate little fingers couldn't find the switch.

Silence.

J: I'm here! I'm here!

K: What is this tincture? Where is it coming from?

J: Oh, jeez! Hell if I know.

K: I'm really very thirsty.

J: That's your body talking. Don't listen to what your body says. Try to cry. Can you cry? Then you can drink your tears and survive indefinitely.

K: I've been crying for weeks. I can't anymore. I am definitely the "no more tears formula." I've drunk every available drop of fluid in my eyes.

J: The light is rapidly disappearing. Don't listen to your body! You've suffered a massive intoxication of aridity, and that has caused a desperate glandular urgency, a desperate urge for …

K: Come to think of it, I have been really horny lately. Water …

J: Isn't there any water in the hotel?

K: Not a drop. The cat is barely moving. It drank my last tear. Is the light on?

J: Yes.

K: Well, I don't see a thing. I've swallowed my eyes.

J: It's the dry season.

K: You're not kidding. What about the helicopter? I'm going to turn the light off; it's cooler that way.

J: Don't listen to your body!

K: The glandular urge for fluids?

J: Leave it on, or we won't be able to see you.

K: I don't care. I can't see myself, so why should you?

J: Wait for the rain.

Gunshot sounds.

K: What rain? What's going on out there?

J: Nothing.

K: What's going on?

J: Just a little argument out here.

K: Who's getting shot?

J: No one.

K: Steve! Are you there?

J: Yes.

K: What's wrong?

J: Nothing.

K: Where is everyone? Joe? Maria? Claudia?! Anyone there?

J: We're here.

K: Steve?

F: Steve's gone for a while. He's been hit.

K: By what?

F: The palpitations that began in the earthquake have spread to our area.

K: But you're so far away!

Explosion sounds.

F: I know.

K: Any water?

F: Get up!

K: I can't. I've just returned to the earth for a moment, but it's just a slight return.

F: Well, return permanently to a vertical position.

K: Get me a helicopter, and I will.

F: And keep that cat moving! It's not moving!

K: So, what does my skin look like?

Gunshot sounds.

10. Just A Little Argument

K: Joe!? Are you there? What's happening?

F: Just a little argument. Hey! Put that down! You can't do that!

K: Do what?

F: Hey! Get away from there! Put that guitar down! Let go of that!

K: Steve? Maria? Joe? Billy Bob?

1: It's just a little argument.

F: Hey! Get out of here!

K: Who is that?

2: We're a voice in the wilderness.

K: Who?

4: *Que se chingan!*

Gunshots sounds.

F: Hey, get out of here!

K: Is anyone there? Steve? Someone call security!

2: We are security.

K: Well, I don't see any badges.

1: We don't need no stinking badges!

K: What is going on out there?

3: You have to go out for a hamburger.

K: Steve, I really think you'd better go out for that hamburger.

F: Put that guitar down. Let go of that!

2: "I didn't mean to take up all your sweet time. I'll give it right back to you one of these days." I said, "I didn't mean to take up all your sweet time. I'll give it right back to you one of these days."

K: Steve? Steve!

4: "If I don't see you no more in this world, I'll meet you in the next one, so don't be late. Don't be late!"

Gunshot. Guitar sounds.

K: Steve? Maria? Joe? Billy Bob?

VOICES 1, 2, 3, 4 sing first verse of "Electric Ladyland," by Jimi Hendrix, a cappella:

"Have you ever been … to Electric Ladyland?" …

K: Steve? Maria? Joe? Billy? Billy Bob?

Hendrix guitars. Silence.

1: Be careful! The molten cloud of your memory is about to explode!

K: Steve?

2: Here it goes!

Violins.

K: Where's Steve?

4: He went out for a hamburger.

K: Well, who the fuck are you?

3: Don't you remember us?

1: From the hotel.

K: I don't remember you at the hotel.

2: Don't you remember us?

4: We left you standing there a long time ago.

K: Well, get me the fuck out of here, then!

3: You never said she was such a bitch!

K: Who you callin' a bitch?!

1: Uhhh … no one. Jesus fucking Christ, girl!

2: We won't leave you here.

K: Did you bring the helicopter?

4: There is no helicopter.

K: Where is everybody?

3: They went out for a hamburger.

1: We are everybody now.

K: Identify yourselves.

2: Mr. Tizayucan.

4: Mr. Huehuetoca.

3: Mr. Tlalneplantla.

1: Mr. Tequisquiac.

K: Fat chance! What are you, Japanese or something?

2: No, no, no! Vieja bruta! We are from the Casa Negra. We are here to help you out.

K: Then where's the fucking door?!

4: There is no fucking door. There is only the sky.

K: What good does that do me?

3: Don't worry. Magic is everywhere around you.

K: Where are the other everybodies?

1: They left you standing here a long time ago.

2: But we have returned, slightly.

4: To turn the beat around, like that song.

3: We have to hurry now. The Casa Negra is about to explode!

1: Who did you say you were?

2: There are four of us, like the Beatles.

K: Who are you, the four horsemen?

4: A long, long time ago. Do you remember?

1, 2, 3, and 4 argue in Spanish.

K: Hey, guys! Guys!

1: Yes? You do remember?

K: Who are you?

2: We told you!

4: The volcano will convulse until it is satisfied. We are at its command, so let's get the fuck out of here, lady!

3: We're leaving.

K: Hey! Wait!

1: Hell no!

K: Which way?

3: Up!

4: You have to go up twenty-five more floors!

K: But I'm on the roof!

3: Turn your feet around and let's get out of here! How?

1: Walking.

2: Running.

4: Flying.

3: Rising.

K: How?

1: I'm trying to tell you to get up! You have to get up there, man!

K: Who are you?

2: We told you.

K: How can I be sure?

3: We don't need no stinking badges!

K: Somebody get me a cheeseburger!

2: Now get up!

4: Get the fuck up!

2: Shake your groove thing, and let's get out the hell out of here!

4: Are you coming?

3: *Cadajo!* It's going to blow!

K: All right!

1: Then turn the beat around, and let's get the fuck out of here! *Andalé, cabronsita!*

Rain.

11. Nectar

K: It's a nectar of some sort. The dirt on my face has turned into a nectar. It's gone through some sort of convoluted ionization.

> *March 1*
> Dear Maria,
> Once you sent me a postcard of a black, ugly mountain, saying that you felt it described your feeling of darkness, how you hated everything. Now I send you the same one with the same message. When I saw your card, I doubted its ugliness; but

then I'd never seen it from the inside. I've discovered that I'm not at the top of the hotel, as I once thought, but somewhere in the lower third. And it's not a hotel at all, but a dwarf volcano occupying the former location of the hotel.

March 9
The hotel has changed. I must get to the upper chamber of the volcano before it goes through another convulsion. The moist cloud of your memory comes back to me in drops of molten black liquid. We can sense the scent of the volcano's nectar here inside the dwarf planet. The cat fears another convulsion. I've met four other scientists, or they say they are. They never talk about science, but of the five directions available to us. I suppose I'll have to believe them. They don't appear to be lost. They live in the volcano hotel with great ease and seem to have been there for quite some time. They know its history better than I do, even further back than the first human occupation of the Casa Negra. They've promised to lead me out, sooner or later, but to do that we must climb what seems like miles of rock formations. The cat is very weak, but refuses to be carried.

March 14
Before we started climbing up further than the eleventh floor, they helped me bury Claudia in the bank vault of the Casa Negra.

March 19
I'll miss the pool and the ice cream. I don't see any light above; but they say we won't see the opening for quite some time, perhaps weeks, we are so far down.

March 30
Sometimes dead birds fall downward past us at amazing
speeds. That is the only way we can tell we are going up; although once a huge flock of blue cranes flew up from far below
and then disappeared in the black above us. What the hell were
they doing down there? Messengers escaping from the dead
city. Living birds never fly down toward us.

April 28
We have now reached the thirty-fifth floor. Still nothing. I'm beginning to think the four scientists don't know where we are going. I suppose we're going up. The air seems a bit brighter, clearer.
The tincture on my body seems to be fading slowly. I'll miss it.

May 30
The cat has revived, somewhat. It's changing colors. Its tongue
has started to grow back, and it's stuttering faint sounds that
sound like "Mama, Mama." But it never needed a tongue to
talk anyway.

June 15
At last we reach thirty-eight. Still nothing.

July 4
Sorry I haven't written. What are we eating? Nothing, I suppose. The cat won't stop talking. It really won't shut up. It's
driving us all crazy.

August 19
We've reached the forty-fifth floor. It seems a bit brighter,
but still no real light. By now it seems obvious that the four
scientists had miscalculated the depth. We are now thirty-four

floors above the original eleven floors of the Casa Negra. They
said there were twenty-five more above us; but who knows
how many are left. The tincture has almost disappeared.

August 30
Fifty-fifth floor. Still nothing. The tincture has disappeared .
But so has the cat. It left a note promising to return.

September12
Sixty-fourth floor. Still no cat, no light.

September 29
That damned cat still hasn't come back. Where the hell is it?
My companions are worried and starting to argue among
themselves. But it does seem a bit brighter. My body seems
lighter.

October 16
We counted fifty-eight dead birds falling by today, all of different colors. But still no cat. By the way, we're on the seventy-
ninth floor.

October 30
Eighty-sixth floor.

November 14
Very little progress. Eighty-eighth floor, and I'm ready to stop
counting.

November 28
Maybe we're really going down. Ninety-second floor. It's getting brighter. Still nothing above us but blue-black.

December 1
The cat has returned. Disguised in a small elephant mask.
Ninety-ninth floor. It says it nearly reached the top, but has
no idea how many more floors there are. I never taught it to
count, and now I regret it. Floor ninety-three. No birds today.

December 8
Floor ninety-four. Very rough going.

December 14
My sister's birthday. My four friends have split up. Three have
gone in different directions. Tequisquiac has remained with us,
and we will go in the fourth direction. Floor ninety-seven.

December 24
We are beginning to feel a cool moisture from above rather
than the heat from below. But still not much progress. Floor
ninety-nine, and no sign of our three friends. Where the fuck
are we?

December 29
Tlalnepantla has returned. In his direction he found only darkness. Floor 106.

January 15
Anyway, Tizayucan and Huehuetoca have returned together.
They crossed paths. Both had gone upwards, but found each
other on the eleventh floor, where we buried Claudia. So we
continue in the fourth direction.

January 29

We have been tormented for three days by continuous rain-storms. But they're coming from below us. We felt a convul-sion below us. Have initiated swimming lessons for the group.

February 9

The rains have stopped. The cat is in a sour mood. Insists that we go in a totally different direction. Have lost all count of what floor we're on.

February 27

More convulsions. A dead goat flew by us today. We ate it. Yes, it was raw.

February 29

It's gotten much brighter. I calculate that we are on the 125th floor. An insect of some kind flew by today. But it wouldn't fly any lower than we were.

March 16

The insect has returned. We're following it quickly in the direc-tion of what appears to be a speck of light.

March 19

Hundred-and-thirty-sixth floor, I think. The speck of light has gotten bigger. The insect, which turns out to be some sort of a flea, is still with us. Maybe it's attracted by the cat.

March 20

We are nearer the opening. We can see birds overhead. The flea has gone.

March 30

Another convulsion from below us; a bit of smoke and debris
from below us. The contents of the kitchen of the Casa Negra
floated past us in a violent sunburst of guacamole. I thought I
saw Claudia's shoes fly by us. Who knows?

I just realized that once we get to the top, we're going to have
to climb down this damn thing anyway. And what's out there
when we get there?

April 4

The scientists are saying that this isn't the volcano they origi-
nally entered. It's totally different, not the dwarf volcano we
thought it was. The cat agrees, so I agree.

April 9

We reach the top today. The volcano is not huge, as we
thought. Not even a dwarf volcano, but a midget volcano.
We're ten feet off the ground. It's an anthill.

April 10

We camped out on the top. Afraid to move in any direction.

April 11

Today we split up. Each of the four scientists went in a different direction. The cat and I will head in the fifth.

And so we go, until hopefully we can find Highway 61. Goodbye, Claudia. I'm sorry we had to leave you down there so
deep. But this is what people do to each other. This is what
people do for each other when that is all they can do for each
other. This is what people do to themselves when they can't
do for themselves. We can still smell the nectar of the volcano
on our bodies And so I still wait for my baby to return, even

if only slightly. When east goes west, when west goes east, and south north, north south. Like that, just like that, even if only slightly.

Screens flash momentarily and go black.

Shatterhand Massacree. Left to right: Sanghi Wagner, Michael Tighe, Steve Buscemi. Photo: Kirk Winslow.

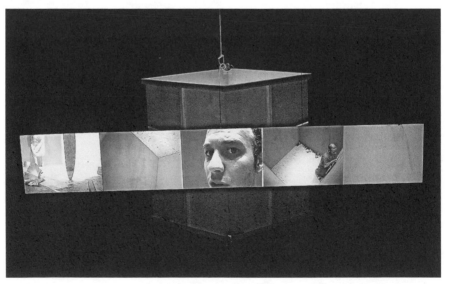

Slight Return. Ari Brickman in a scene from the performance. Photo: John Jesurun.

Snow. Mary Ewald in a scene from the performance. Photo: John Jesurun.

Firefall. Left to right: Claire Buckingham, Ray Roy, Alex Anfanger, Stephanie Silver.
Photo: Paula Court.

☐ SCREENS

▨ PERFORMING AREA - HALLWAYS, 4 ROOMS

■ AUDIENCE

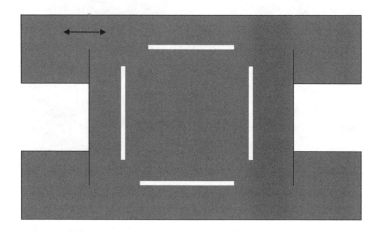

AUDIENCE AREA - 24 X 24 FT.
ROOMS- 12 X 12 FT.
SCREENS- 9 X 12 FT.
HALLS 6FT. WIDE
SIDE VIEW

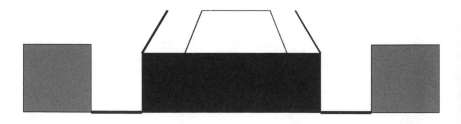

Snow. Floor plan by the author. Photo: John Jesurun.

Snow

For William Harris

Snow premiered November 9, 2000, at the First Christian Church, Seattle, Washington. It was produced by the New City Theater (John Kazanjian, Producer) and Shatterhand. Support was provided by Rockefeller MAP Funds, the BAM/Lucent Arts in Multimedia Program, and the Flintridge Foundation. Community support was provided by Media 911, Staging Techniques, Shawn Brinsfield, and On the Boards.

Cast

4 live actors, 22 cameras, 1 virtual actor
CRICKETT/MILDRED PIERCE/CONCHITA: Valerie Charles
INTERN: Peter Sorensen
KIT/CZARINA: Mary Ewald
BALLOU: Jojo Abaoag
LEE/MONTE BERAGON: Peter Crook

Rebecca Moore, Black Beetle/Michael Tighe: *Music*
Ben Geffen: *Technical Director/Lighting Design*
Tim Coulter: *Video Technical Director*
Dan Lee: *Virtual Actor Program Designer*
Bill Ballou: *Entity Track Design*
Kit August: *Media Consultant*
Kelly Wilbur: *Media Manager*
Mike Taylor: *Technical Coordinator, Lucent Project*

Written, directed, and designed by John Jesurun

Characters

CRICKETT: Actress. Early forties.
BALLOU: Television executive, male. Late thirties.
KIT: Senior television executive, female. Early forties.
BALLOU: Television writer, blind. Mid-twenties.
INTERN: Seventeen. (Camera.)

Set Description

Interior: *The audience sits within an enclosed center area that is twenty-four feet square. The room seats seventy-five people. The walls are nine feet high. Inside, the carpeted floor and walls are dark blue. Four nine-by-twelve-foot screens, one above each wall, slant downward at forty-five-degree angles towards the audience. The audience enters through a passageway from the lobby. For the performance, this passage folds into two doors that are closed and made flush with the walls of the viewing area. Two small windows in these doors occasionally reveal action on the outside as actors walk by. The audience is completely separated from the live action.*

Exterior: *Directly on the other side of the wall surrounding the audience area are four six-foot-wide hallways that connect four rooms, each on a corner of the outside space. Each room is about twelve feet square. All of the live action takes place within this outside space. Four live actors on radio microphones inhabit the halls and rooms during the performance. The action is transmitted to the screens in the center viewing area by twenty cameras placed throughout the acting space. Two cameras are manned by operators. The rest are in fixed positions, except for the computerized camera (INTERN). The twenty camera views, as well as prerecorded material, are in a constant state of live edit on the four screens. All live sound is transmitted to speakers inside the viewing area. A track is suspended from the outside wall of the viewing space. The computerized camera runs on this track and is able to circle the hallway almost completely. Its movements along the track can be controlled by an operator in the control room. The camera is also programmed to move by itself, to recognize, focus, pan, and tilt, according to whom it is programmed to follow. This camera entity represents the speaking, but unseen, fifth character (INTERN) in the piece. This character/camera (virtual actor) has a voice accompaniment. Room 1 serves as the real-life technical control room for the piece. Lights, sound, video computers, and technicians are all in this room. This room also serves as the control room in the "play." Room 2 is a dressing room; Room 3, a*

living room; Room 4, an office. Other action takes place in the hallways.
The views of the four screens are constantly changing and showing other
views, as well as the "scene" indicated by the text.

1.

Camera moves slowly to close-up of Crickett *in Japanese costume and*
makeup. She speaks in a bad Japanese accent.

Crickett: Once I lived in a holy city. It was a bright city, a holy city. It lay
under a beautiful dark silver cloud with no lining. The cloud was solid,
impenetrable, a holy iceberg floating in the sky. It covered the whole city
from end to end for many miles. Sometimes the cloud would descend
upon the entire city for days and take hundreds of people with it. And
so in many ways it seemed that it was a city half dead and half alive. It
had been like this for a century. Because it existed in this middle state, it
remained the holiest city. It was well known that half the city was on its
way to the other world. And so the inhabitants became very delicate and
wise in their ways. Many left in fear of the cloud. But many more came
to live in its holy shadow. They would spend hours looking at the sky …
wondering. As it began its second century, the city began to lose its holiness and depth and became a vain and narrow city, and the cloud began
to dissipate. Each time it descended, it took fewer and fewer people.
Finally it dropped one last time without taking anyone, and vanished.
The emperor was distraught, and he tried to get it back. He couldn't bear
his city without its silver cloud. But the cloud never returned. The city
had become unworthy of its cloud and its holiness—and I with it. It was
now in fact an unholy city. After fifty years, the emperor died without
ever finding the cloud, and his family fell into dishonor. Many left to
look for another cloud. They either died on their long journeys, or they
came back very old, with a look of heartache in their eyes. Like me,
they came back to wait it out. I must satisfy myself with small clumps
of clouds and thunderstorms. I see a white cloud, and I want it to turn

black. The city is rich and beautiful now, but it's full of empty people, and any mention of the holy city is ridiculed. I look inside myself and see my heart is black. And so slowly the holy city became was destroyed, disappeared, ... and vanished to nothing but dust on the desert plain. And it did this through its own stubborn will and its winning ways. And that's how it was. I became what I am there. And so now I am just an old woman sifting through the dust of what was once a holy city ... Cut! ... Ugh! *(Crickett breaks character and storms off set to her dressing room. She begins taking off her makeup and costume.)* Will someone please tell me what that was supposed to mean? Someone, please, what was that about?! No, don't tell me. I don't want to know. Anyway. How was that? Good? Great. I'm going home now, and don't call me. What time tomorrow? For what? I thought that was the last scene, right? The finale? Looping and pickup shots ... okay, okay! ... *(Pulls off wig.)* And what is this wig made out of anyway?!

2.

Lee and Intern in control room.

INTERN: ... Well, what is that increment?

LEE: I don't know, and neither do they.

INTERN: What do you mean, they don't know?

LEE: They don't know. It's not their department.

INTERN: Why?

LEE: It's someone else's.

INTERN: Where is the third function?

LEE: There is no third function—that we know of.

INTERN: Well, how do I edit it without knowing what the third function is?

LEE: You're just the intern, you don't have to edit it. We just take care of it up to this point. Then it goes on to the next department, and they take care of it.

INTERN: Who's in that department?

LEE: Look, just proofread the damn thing and send it out. The censors will fix it later if they have to.

INTERN: What is this miniseries about?

LEE: The description says, "When Southern charm turns into plantation owners and slave drivers."

INTERN: What?

LEE: That's all they gave us. That's all it says. Who cares? And it has to stay that way. The punctuation has to be exact.

INTERN: Exactly what?

LEE: Exactly that, and don't change a period, because you'll get fired if you do.

INTERN: I just want to change one thing.

LEE: Don't touch it.

INTERN: Jesus. Okay.

LEE: Let me see that. It's fine. Now send it out, and go get me some coffee.

INTERN: All right.

3.

CRICKETT's dressing room.

CRICKETT: *(On phone.)* Darling, I'm going to put you on the speakerphone for just a few minutes ... Uh-huh. Then it says ... "There must be no crying because then the soul will become attached and want to stay to comfort the living ... " ... Anyway, then her husband dies and leaves her alone ... It's so obvious ... The intern wrote it ... They'll never use it here—it's not bad enough ... Let's see ... "But then the city became unholy—and I with it." Isn't that from that other show? ... Then the servant says: "It was a pity, but there is no room for pity ..." ... Blah blah ... Then the pharaoh's wife says: "I had to separate myself from myself so I could watch out for myself day by day. And I do ... in a stuporific stupor." But enough of the poetics ... Let's see, this must be the new scene ... What is this? Oh, listen to this ... "Time to be between a rock and another hard rock. Goddamn the rock that will not roll." I don't know how they expect me to say things like this ... "God pity a rock that can gather no moss, for in its dryness it will crumble. But crumbling is to be honored—even admired." Blah blah blah ... Then I jump into the river ... Yeah ... I sent the check yesterday! ... I can't. I have all this memorizing to do! Get this ... The pharaoh says: "Soon will be the time when everything will be taken away from you and you from everything ..."And so on and so on ... Blah blah blah ... Here's a good one ... Then I as his blind mother say: "I beheld the earth, and lo, it was waste and void. And the heavens. And they had no light. I beheld the mountains, and lo, they trembled." It's too heavy for me. Then the princess Nefertiri finally says: "The eye of the monkey is upon you." Yeah, right ... (CRICKETT *hangs up.*)

4.

LEE and BALLOU in LEE's office.

LEE: We need a story about a slave owner, some kind of plantation thing.

BALLOU: I know. I read the prospectus.

LEE: Can you write sitcoms?

BALLOU: No.

LEE: Can you try to come up with some dummy scenes for us? We just need the text and some kind of idea for the scene setups based on what we gave you. Could you make all the scenes interiors?

BALLOU: What about the plantation story?

LEE: Can you have three dummies by tomorrow at ten? Just dummy them up. They won't be used for anything. We just want to see what you can do.

BALLOU: But I don't write sitcoms.

LEE: You'll really be helping us out with this. Don't worry, you're still on the miniseries. You'd be doing me a big favor. I'm trying to get a jump on things here. You'll be paid $3,000 for each one-minute dummy. Just whip something up.

BALLOU: I'll try.

LEE: Good. And only work on the computer we provided you with. Remember, you can only do work-related writing on it. So don't use it for anything else. No personal e-mail, no poetry, no personal correspondence. All corrections will come from the tenth floor two days following your submissions by company e-braille. You have to respond in twenty-four hours to any suggestions or corrections. It's all in your contract renewal, which I hope you read.

BALLOU: It's five hundred pages. I'll have to download it.

LEE: It won't download. It's company property, and it will automatically be deleted in two days. All information in the contract is confidential, but that's normal.

5.

CRICKETT, LEE, and KIT in KIT's office.

CRICKETT: ... But what do you mean? Do you think I'm a mediocre actress?

LEE: *(To KIT.)* Do you think she's a mediocre actress?

KIT: No. Well, not mediocre, but sort of regular … I mean good, but mid-range … not great, but okay … But that's all right. Nothing wrong with that … I mean she's good for this … She is under exclusive contract.

LEE: I mean, she can't be that bad. What do you make? A few million a year?

CRICKETT: Why are you asking me this?

LEE: Actually, Crickett, you are mediocre. You just are. But dependable.

KIT: But that's okay. We need that. We want that. That's why we'd like you in management.

CRICKETT: If I'm so mediocre, why am I in so many of these productions?

LEE: The company is hungry, and it must be fed.

CRICKETT: What about the audience?

KIT: "Them belly full but they hungry."*

CRICKETT: A hungry mob is a hungry mob. What about that Beckett project we did?

KIT: It was a crock … Come on. We don't care if they see it or not.

CRICKETT: All that work for nothing?

LEE: Nothing is never not for nothing

CRICKETT: But I don't want to be in management. I want to act.

KIT: You call that acting?

CRICKETT: Kit, what does that mean?

LEE: Well, you are a mediocre actress, and you can stay that way if you want. We can always use you. I just thought you might like to move in a different direction.

CRICKETT: I like it where I am.

---

* From "Them Belly Full," by Bob Marley.

KIT: You do?

LEE: Don't you want to know more about how we do things?

CRICKETT: No.

KIT: How long have you been here?

CRICKETT: Fifteen years.

LEE: You've been here fifteen years and you don't want to know?

CRICKETT: What is there to know?

KIT: Actors are usually pretty ... and pretty stupid, but we know you aren't.

CRICKETT: Mediocre, but not stupid.

KIT: Right.

CRICKETT: I couldn't be any more mediocre than the scripts you give me.

LEE: So why do them anymore?

6.

LEE guides BALLOU through company hallway.

LEE: The dummies were all right. Now we want you to rewrite them.

BALLOU: What about the slave story?

LEE: Save that for later; it would be great to have the dummies now. You saw the suggestions?

BALLOU: Yes.

LEE: Sitcom number one has to have the words: red, blue, dog, elaborate, never, only, and because, and all the other words on list A. The main characters' names are Alice and Brian. You can't use the words if, car, carrot, carve, cartwheel, or won't. So strike those and the other four hundred words on list B.

BALLOU: Why ?

LEE: No big reason. That's just the form we request. Think of it as a writing exercise. Can you have it this afternoon by five?

BALLOU: I think so.

LEE: Come back at five and we'll go over it again. Don't worry about any action directives. We'll take care of that.

BALLOU: What about music, Mr. Lee?

LEE: The music department will take care of that. Don't worry about going out for lunch. Just call the service number. They'll deliver whatever you want.

BALLOU: I thought I could work at home.

LEE: Maybe next week. You don't mind. We're under a lot of pressure right now. You understand. Did you finish reading your contract renewal?

BALLOU: I had to call a lawyer.

LEE: You can use our lawyer. She'll help you.

BALLOU: I didn't like her.

LEE: She didn't like you either, but she'll help you.

BALLOU: I'd rather use my own.

LEE: That's fine. Now go and finish those dummies, you little dummy.

7.

CRICKETT and WALLY FAY in CRICKETT's dressing room. The character of WALLY FAY is played by the actor who plays BALLOU.

CRICKETT: I'm so glad you're going to join us. What's your name?

WALLY: Wally, Wally Fay.

CRICKETT: You're going to do things here you haven't even imagined yet. I'm going to tell you a few things. It's just some advice about how we work here. Is that okay? The first rule I learned is that everything you say here must be written by someone else. Never say anything you think or write yourself. In fact, never put anything down in writing—you never know where it will end up. Next, you always want what they want, and they want what you want, and everything will go perfectly. Is this being taped?

LEE: *(LEE's voice on speaker.)* Yes, it is, and it has been recorded.

CRICKETT: I thought so. Do you understand me?

WALLY: Yes.

CRICKETT: No, you don't. You don't understand me .You're just saying you do because you want the job. That's your first mistake. Is that why you're saying you understand me when you don't?

WALLY: Yes.

CRICKETT: Wrong answer. You'll have to leave. This isn't the place for you. You won't like it here.

WALLY: Why?

CRICKETT: Wrong question. I'm sorry, it just won't work out.

WALLY: But why? It was all set.

CRICKETT: You're a method writer, aren't you?

WALLY: Yes.

CRICKETT: Well, I don't work with method writers. You understand, it wouldn't work out. Different strokes. Goodbye and good luck.

Wally leaves.

LEE: Where did he go?

CRICKETT: He won't be working here. Call in the next one.

Ballou enters in different clothes.

CRICKETT: What's your name?

BALLOU: Steve, Steve Harrington, but you can call me Ballou.

CRICKETT: I'm so glad you're going to join us.

BALLOU: Me too.

CRICKETT: Sit down … I'm going to tell you a few things. It's just some advice about how we work here. Is that okay? Some of it you may not understand yet, but eventually you will. The first rule I learned is that everything you say here must be written by someone else … Next, you always want what they want, and they want what you want, and everything will go perfectly. Do you understand me?

BALLOU: No.

CRICKETT: Yes, you do, you do understand me. Look at my face! Do you want to look like this some day? See what it's done to me?! Do you want to turn into a creep?! Do you want to be totally outside of yourself?! Drawn and quartered?! Raked over the coals? Lose everything you ever thought was yours to get what you never wanted in the first place?!

BALLOU: No.

CRICKETT: Then you'll do fine here. We'll see you tomorrow.

8.

CRICKETT *in her dressing room with* INTERN.

CRICKETT: Well, I had a shocking day today.

INTERN: I can imagine.

CRICKETT: It's that death scene I had to read at the auditions today. We had to audition twenty-seven actors for the character of my husband. I died twenty-seven deaths in four hours.

INTERN: I thought you already had an actor.

CRICKETT: Oh, he died a month ago. I can't do this. But unfortunately I can do this so I guess I will do it. So I guess I'll have to. I had to do it even though I didn't want to—but that's all right So, all right, I had to die twenty-seven times today, and I'm sick of it. But that's all right. I tell you, I was withered at the end of the day.

BALLOU: *(Passing in hallway.)* There's a call for you on line six.

INTERN: Don't bother her, she died twenty-seven times today.

BALLOU: She looks like it.

CRICKETT: This is the third miniseries I've died in, and I'm sick of it.

INTERN: But you're so good at it.

CRICKETT: Won't we all be. Anyway, what's happening tomorrow?

INTERN: Costume fitting and makeup consultations.

CRICKETT: It ain't nothin' but a heartache.

INTERN: Auditions at five …

CRICKETT: Please don't tell me they didn't find an actor for my husband. I won't die one more time in that audition room, I won't do it!

INTERN: This is for your daughter's part.

CRICKETT: She's not in the death scene, is she? She can't be.

INTERN: She's not.

CRICKETT: Otherwise I'll go ape-shit. Who is writing these scripts anyway? They don't make any sense. They've got to stop hiring those Yale graduates. What do they know about death anyway? … Ape-shit, I tell you.

9.

INTERN's voice over.

INTERN: The main actress I'm assisting here is a ball of confusion. Sending out so many signals at once that I never know what she's thinking. She's an amazing creature. She's a living encryption in a universe of mixed messages. But it works well on the screen. Now I've learned to do the same thing. And so I plant seeds of doubt wherever I can. I can imply so many things at once that either everyone will trust me, or no one will trust me. She told me several times that I was walking on thin ice, but I think we've learned to trust each other.

10.

CRICKETT *and* INTERN *in hallway.*

CRICKETT: *(To* INTERN *as they walk down hallway.)* The first show I did here I met an actor named Ed. He seemed nice enough, and we got along well. I had hoped he wasn't evil. I cried on his shoulder and put my confidence in him. I soon learned not to trust actors as far as I could throw myself at them. He was a horrible person, but a wonderful actor, and after a while I couldn't stand it anymore, so I thought I'd try to get him fired, but before I could do it that big queen in administration did it. Why? Not because Ed was a jerk, but because his acting was too good. It's been the same with every good actor that's come in here. I've outlasted all of them, and I'm beginning to wonder why.

11.

CRICKETT *on spaceship set in space costume. The other character in this scene is played by the actor who plays* LEE. *Pre-recorded.*

LEE: Don't search for signs of life around here; everything and everyone is neutered, neutral, and neutralized. It's the way of the world, so get with it or get under it, but don't try to get out of it.

CRICKETT: But I don't want to be neutralized.

LEE: Be that as it may, it is as it should be, and it will be what it should be. You have to know your place in the universe. Learn to be nothing, and be nothing happily ever after, as I have.

CRICKETT: But how have you already learned to be nothing?

LEE: Because my soul is in my brain. It's a process of moving your soul to your brain.

CRICKETT: Easy come, easy go?

LEE: Forget about seeing the world as it could be—see it as it is and stop crying. Crying is an exercise in humiliating futility.

CRICKETT: And so I must not cry. I don't know why, but I seem to cry at almost anything these days.

LEE: Is there anything else I can do for you? Your gravestone. How do you want to be remembered?

CRICKETT: I don't want to be remembered; I'd like to be forgotten. Someone who's done all the useless things I've done should be forgotten.

LEE: Like I said, you have to know your place in the universe, and this is not it. (*LEE shoots CRICKETT with space gun. She falls dead.*)

12.

BALLOU, CRICKETT, and LEE walking down hallway.

BALLOU: I think it's weird that everything is seen through the eyes of the first person, the narrator.

CRICKETT: Why?

BALLOU: Because as the narrator, the author tells the story, and sees everything, and knows everyone's thoughts. But while it's happening he watches and never does anything to interrupt the action, no matter how awful it is. He just sits there and tells you what happens. He's there, and he never gets involved. How can he just sit there and watch a murder, and not do anything to stop it?! He's the audience of one pretending to be the audience of none. I hate narrators! They know everything and never do anything about it. They just tell the story while the whole world goes down the drain!

LEE: Chill out and forget about all that. I just want to make sure we have this right. The previous scene is her in her apartment and …

BALLOU: She is alone, and she is looking at a photograph of him.

LEE: And she's wearing a red blouse, right?

BALLOU: Why does it have to be red?

LEE: It just does. Then the narrator says ...

BALLOU: Then the narrator says: "He saw that she was alone, but he saw such astonishing beauty in her that he was scarcely able to contain himself at the sight ... To see—in the depth of the night, in the loveliest spot in the world—to see the person whom he adored, to see her without her knowing that she was seen, and to see her entirely occupied with matters relating to himself ... is something no other lover has ever enjoyed or imagined."*

CRICKETT: Why does something so beautiful have to turn into something so ugly?

BALLOU: The idea here is: Is it possible to protest? ... to speak up? ... to fight back?

CRICKETT: To kill back? To not remain silent? That's not how it is in the book.

LEE: Don't you understand? She kills him. That is her answer. A killer is a killer, and killers must be killed by killers, and so she kills him and becomes a killer.

CRICKETT: But why do I kill him? And how am I supposed to kill him?! He's too tall!

LEE: Oh, just kill him.

CRICKETT: All right. I'll kill him. Why should I care why?

LEE: Kill, please. Don't wonder why ...

CRICKETT: (Leaving.) Thank you ...

---

* From The Princess of Clèves, by Madame de La Fayette.

13.

CRICKETT on set. On screen we see her strangling someone from the point of view of the VICTIM. When the unseen VICTIM speaks, it has the voice of the INTERN.

CRICKETT: *(She walks up to the camera/VICTIM. She struggles as she strangles her VICTIM. She steps back, staring into the camera.)* … It's a certain kind of tenderness … Why have I let it come to this? God said to Abraham, kill me a son, and I did. I folded him into a cloud … I had to put him out of the way, but I didn't want to. I was happy when he became quiet and lay there still. I had to shut his electric eye forever, and now his love is blind. But everyone knows an eye never stops seeing. Did it really shut down, or does it keep seeing afterwards? Maybe he's still looking at me with that dis-encrypted eye. At first he could just see me. Now he can see through me, but I don't care. Because now I don't have to see him seeing me. *(CRICKETT grabs a sandwich and begins eating it as she speaks.)* Now I can finally eat my lunch in peace. Thank God, no more of that staring at me, creeping me out, asking questions, hanging around outside the door. He was everywhere. I couldn't get rid of him. I couldn't stand him looking at me. One less thing to worry about. My heart has turned black, black, black … from being watched, watched, watched … all, all, all, the time, time … time. Wouldn't yours?

VICTIM: Mine hasn't.

CRICKETT: Yours was black to begin with. The constant choreography of your eye was destroying me.

VICTIM: I've turned into a red skeleton flapping in the wind.

CRICKETT: Killing you was the only thing I could do that really meant something, and now I see that it means nothing at all because you meant nothing at all to me. But I didn't realize that until after I killed you.

VICTIM: You only hurt the ones you love.

CRICKETT: I don't love you! What am I talking to you for anyway? You're not even real. I thought I just killed you.

VICTIM: You didn't. You killed yourself.

CRICKETT: I did not! This was a murder scene, not a suicide scene.

VICTIM: It's been changed.

CRICKETT: Stop looking at me.

VICTIM: I can't.

CRICKETT: Then I'll have to unplug you again. (CRICKETT *begins strangling* VICTIM *again.)*

VICTIM: No! Don't!!

LEE: *(On speaker.)* ... And fade out. Beautiful.

CRICKETT: What an awful scene. Please don't tell me I have to do it again. How could someone write such awful, idiotic thoughts? Shame on you, Ballou!

BALLOU: *(On speaker.)* It wasn't my idea.

LEE: It's a psycho-thriller for the Japanese market.

CRICKETT: Dubbed?

LEE: Subtitles.

CRICKETT: Oh forget it. I don't want to know.

14.

CRICKETT, LEE, and Kit in restaurant.

CRICKETT: ... You know, I think you're right. I should go into producing. I'm getting tired of all of this.

KIT: But you don't have to ... You can act.

CRICKETT: I thought you wanted me to produce?

LEE: We thought about it again, and we realize we need you as an actress. We'll raise your salary and get you better scripts.

KIT: We know you had an offer from another studio.

CRICKETT: No one knew that! How did you know?

LEE: So we'll double their offer.

CRICKETT: I'm not worth that much, and you know it.

LEE: To us you are.

CRICKETT: Let me talk to the other studio. They're giving me better scripts.

KIT: We acquired those scripts from them for you.

CRICKETT: Already? I'm beginning to feel claustrophobic.

LEE: Open a window.

KIT: We can do another Chekhov thing.

CRICKETT: So no one will watch it? And the ones who do will watch a mediocre actress doing great scripts. Why would they want to see that? I'm a TV actress. Why should I do Chekhov? I'd like to, but you know I really can't handle it. I'm just good enough for the junk, so I'll do the junk; but I want the best junk around.

LEE: Just tell us what you want. The contract will be ready tomorrow.

CRICKETT: Do we have to sign it so soon?

KIT: The sooner we sign it, the sooner we can start with the new projects.

CRICKETT: What projects?

LEE: Here's a list. Take your pick.

CRICKETT: A remake of *Mildred Pierce*? That's sick.

KIT: You'd be great.

CRICKETT: I'm too old.

LEE: Who cares! We'll change it—get older actors.

CRICKETT: It'll play great in retirement homes.

KIT: It's shown worldwide—you know we have the widest satellite distribution. They can even watch you in the space shuttle.

CRICKETT: Is that so?

LEE: What else can we do for you?

CRICKETT: I want that big queen in production administration to stop asking me so many questions about how I work. Why does he have to know? He seems to think everything I do is the company's business, so tell him to back off. I want that in the contract.

LEE: But Mildred …

KIT: We'll fire him.

CRICKETT: Go ahead. Who are these people? They seem to see and know everything. Why is that?

LEE: We'll find out.

KIT: You already know.

LEE: All right, we'll fire the big queen.

KIT: And his wife in makeup, too.

LEE: Didn't know he had a wife.

CRICKETT: All those big queens in upper management have wives. You know that. That's why they take orders so well. Is my house bugged?

LEE: What?

CRICKETT: Did you bug my house?

KIT: Why would we do that?

CRICKETT: I'm not going back there until its debugged. Understand?

LEE: We'll send the tech people there to check it out.

CRICKETT: They should know their way around. Forget the debugging, just put the house on the market. I don't know what's going on, and I don't want to know. Just get me that contract, and on second thought I will do Mildred Pierce. I want the script tomorrow. The original one—and don't let those hacks in yourscript department touch it.

Kɪᴛ: Anything else?

Cʀɪᴄᴋᴇᴛᴛ: I'll let you know.

Lᴇᴇ: Shall we book you a hotel?

Cʀɪᴄᴋᴇᴛᴛ: I'm staying at your house.

Lᴇᴇ: My wife is there.

Cʀɪᴄᴋᴇᴛᴛ: How long has it been since I slept there? Five years? Don't worry, I don't think she ever found out. Tomorrow morning I want all the tapes you made in my house delivered to my dressing room, which, as you know, is also bugged. That dressing room will be too small to accommodate them, so I'll be needing a larger dressing room. It's so cramped in there. On second thought, I should just retire. And who is that creep you hired that follows me everywhere?

Lᴇᴇ: Shall we fire him, too?

Cʀɪᴄᴋᴇᴛᴛ: No, I kind of like him, but who is he? He's like a dog sniffing around in every corner… What's his deal? And why does he talk so funny? Is he some sort of weird foreign intern? You'd better keep an eye on him. Who knows what he's gotten into.

Kɪᴛ: He's not weird.

Cʀɪᴄᴋᴇᴛᴛ: He's weird … even weirdeʀ than that son-of-a-bitch son of yours who has been spending altogetheʀ too much time in that production administrator's office. And I'm sick of working with those awful coordinators. Where do you get them? Can they even read?

Kɪᴛ: What?

Cʀɪᴄᴋᴇᴛᴛ: You know they're stupid and mediocre. I want to work with someone with a heart, oʀ at least a brain.

LEE: What about a weekly show with music? Think about it.

CRICKETT: Mildred will think about it. Goodbye. *(CRICKETT leaves and walks down hallway.)*

LEE: I thought we were going to make her a producer.

KIT: She's escalating everything.

LEE: What do we need her for? She's just a stupid actress. She's not even any good.

KIT: She's good for us.

LEE: She's been here too long—she knows too much. I say we dump her.

KIT: We have to keep her where she is.

LEE: But I don't want her.

KIT: Who cares what you want? They love her. The tone and inflection of her voice happens to be perfect for encryption. Over the years they've developed an impenetrable code around it. She's become her master's voice, and she doesn't even know it.

LEE: They'll have to change the code eventually.

KIT: It'll take them five years to develop a new one.

LEE: We'll help them.

KIT: They don't want our help. Their whole system is clamped to shut out our Piranhascope.

LEE: When did that happen?

KIT: They let us think we were breaking into their system for ten years.

LEE: How did you find out?

KIT: That queen in management told me.

LEE: How did he find out?

KIT: Sleeping with the enemy.

LEE: Jesus, those queens are everywhere.

KIT: Give him a raise and send him out of the country for a while—and his wife, too. I want them out of here tonight. In any case, we'll dump Crickett when the code does change. She's a horrible actress anyway. Did you see what she did to that Beckett show?

LEE: She's turned into a real pill.

KIT: Cyanide.

LEE: I thought you went to school together.

KIT: Actors Studio and all. I'm sick of her.

LEE: How does she know so much? … Unless you told her.

KIT: Shut up and let's get out of here.

LEE: Check, please …

15.

CRICKETT in her dressing room. LEE and INTERN's voices on speaker.

CRICKETT: Well, I had a shocking day. Shocking, I tell you.

LEE: But why, darling, why?

CRICKETT: Everything seems so fragile—ready to fall apart at any minute. Everyone slowly falling apart all the time—bit by bit. Are we all falling apart? Is that what it is? The deterioration?

LEE: Now, don't get hysterical, dear.

INTERN: Let her get hysterical, let her get it out of her system.

LEE: So let her go ape-shit.

CRICKETT: Don't let me go ape-shit.

LEE: Go on, go ahead … Get it out of your system …

16.

Studio shoot. CRICKETT *begins singing song to camera.*

CRICKETT: *(Singing.)*

> "If you see me, if you please me. Comin' round a Basset Hound
> you must remember felled by slender legs I'm waking look
> what I'm taking Merry go round, begging me.
> Fallen monster red and lonely lying in a darkened chest of
> drawers all over hundreds of them carcassed in their lonely
> autumn begging me to turn him down."*

LEE: *(In control room.)* … And fade out. That's great, Crickett , thank you.
Let's move on to the next one …

17.

CRICKETT *and* INTERN *in her dressing room.*

CRICKETT: Tell her that the dress is too big and—I'd like a triple Karmalatte. With a sugar on the side. On the side, now—not in it, but on the
side.

INTERN: Where did you come from?

CRICKETT: What kind of a question is that?

INTERN: I don't know. Just wondering.

CRICKETT: Look, just go get me a coffee and then you can go … Go now!

INTERN: Regular?

CRICKETT: Triple Karmalatte!! … I came from a small town in California …

INTERN: How did you start acting?

CRICKETT: Go get my coffee, please, I have to wake up. We're shooting in
fifteen minutes.

---

* "If You See Me," by Rebecca Moore.

INTERN: All right. How does it end?

CRICKETT: I don't know, I never got that far.

INTERN: Aren't you interested?

CRICKETT: Not really. I used to be, but now I just learn my own lines. Someone usually tells me eventually.

INTERN: Don't you watch the shows?

CRICKETT: No, I've never seen one of my own pictures.

INTERN: Never?

CRICKETT: Well once, but I was so horrified that I never did again.

INTERN: Why?

CRICKETT: It was awful seeing myself go through all of that.

INTERN: All of what?

CRICKETT: All of the suffering and happiness and the feelings and the face-making and fakery.

INTERN: Don't you enjoy it?

CRICKETT: I enjoy acting out suffering, but seeing myself do it is too painful.

INTERN: It was so sad when you got killed.

CRICKETT: What do you mean, I got killed?

INTERN: You get shot at the end.

CRICKETT: No I don't.

INTERN: Yes you do.

CRICKETT: No I don't. I remember the last scene, and I did not get shot. I shot someone … I think the name of the character was Jim—or was that the actor?

INTERN: But I saw the broadcast last night, and you get shot and die at the end.

CRICKETT: They told me I wasn't going to die in this one.

INTERN: It was changed suddenly.

CRICKETT: No one ever tells me anything, but I'm glad they don't. I can't stand knowing my fate in these things.

INTERN: What does it matter? You didn't see it.

CRICKETT: But just knowing I get shot is bad enough—it makes me have bad dreams.

INTERN: Don't take it personally. It's only a movie.

CRICKETT: For you it is. Now that I know I've been shot, it seems like evil bad luck. And I have to live with it. Knowing I've been shot somewhere in the world in everyone's eyes.

INTERN: You've been shot before.

CRICKETT: Honey, I've been strangled, shot, drowned, poisoned, run over—everything. I used to not mind, but now I hate the idea of it. I try never to die in these shows.

INTERN: Get over it.

CRICKETT: Was there much blood?

INTERN: Don't get so morbid.

CRICKETT: I just want to know what the end was like.

INTERN: Just watch it.

CRICKETT: Oh no, I could never watch myself die. How would you like it? The bullet and the damage done?

INTERN: It might be fun. Liberating.

CRICKETT: I don't want to be liberated that way. I suffer with the thought of knowing it. Now, why did you tell me?!

INTERN: You asked me.

CRICKETT: Did I? Are you ever going to get me my coffee? What is this? An interview for *Teen Scream Magazine*?

INTERN: No.

CRICKETT: Go and get me my coffee, and stop asking me questions.

INTERN: I just want to ask you one more thing.

CRICKETT: Are you going to get my coffee, or not?

INTERN: Yes.

CRICKETT: Yes, ma'am.

INTERN: Yes, ma'am.

CRICKETT: Karmalatte!!

18.

Hallway: BALLOU and INTERN.

INTERN: *(Speaking to BALLOU in the hallway.)* … They told her she was going to play the Dowager Empress, and I had to order her Chinese food every day. Buckets of wonton. She's been eating it all week. It's a terrible thing to do, you know. She thinks it's poison, and I have to taste it first. What's that about?

BALLOU: She played the Dowager five years ago and got an Emmy for it. I saw it—it's a piece of shit.

INTERN: I know. It was worse than Shogun.

19.

CRICKETT and BALLOU in CRICKETT's living room.

CRICKETT: Have another drink …

BALLOU: I want to read you the synopsis for the new show.

CRICKETT: Do we have to do it now? … All right.

BALLOU: It goes like this … They package every show to send a specific encryption on a certain broadcast. They make shows, but their real value is in the encrypted message they send. The show itself is secondary. Everyone thinks they're seeing a show, and the real message goes right by them. Only the designated receiver can decipher it. Crickett is the first level, the template. But beneath her are millions of levels and algorithms that must be de-formulated. But they depend on the construction of the show and your peculiar interpretation of it. Every word, color, plot device, actor, and sound is encoded with a specific meaning within a universe of increments. The original show is simultaneously altered as it's being broadcast to remove the message as it's being delivered. That way they can repeat the show and it will appear the same minus the concealed content.

CRICKETT: What are you talking about?

BALLOU: I think the western we just finished had something to do with the ingredients of a cake or something.

CRICKETT: You mean last week's show was a recipe? I thought I was really good in it.

BALLOU: Haven't you wondered why the scripts are so stupid?

CRICKETT: They aren't any stupider than the ones I did for Aaron Spelling.

BALLOU: You've been here fifteen years and you didn't know?

CRICKETT: I thought I was making television shows. I'm stupid and I'm vain and all I think about is myself and my work. Why would I notice anything else?

BALLOU: That plantation melodrama was part of an equation for a bomb. And the screwball comedy was the otherhalf.

CRICKETT: How many messages can they send? What messages? From whom? To where?

BALLOU: Everywhere, everything. All kinds of messages … equations, plans, astrological predictions, love notes, inventions, patents, personal information, musical compositions, bank transfers, kiddie porn, drug movements, espionage, sabotage, E-bombs, bootlegs, gambling, color codes, copyrights, cures. It's a cryptomania.

CRICKETT: What is this?

BALLOU: The intern told me.

CRICKETT: Why would he tell you something like that?

BALLOU: The Russian story was the schedule for the president's visit to Thailand.

CRICKETT: I ask them to do Anna Karenina, and they turn it into a schedule? That was supposed to be the role of my life. Is it some government agency or something?

BALLOU: This place is its own country. On the fiftieth floor you're known as "her master's voice."

CRICKETT: Who is the master?

BALLOU: No one, really. It's an organization—neutral, apolitical, un-prosecutable, immune. It deals with everyone, and everyone deals with it. It serves everyone, and everyone serves it. It's a service. It accepts payment only in information. Money is irrelevant. It collects so much information that it can use it against any possible enemy if it has to; but the idea is never to use it against anyone, just to threaten to use it. Sort of a neutral Swiss thing.

On the seventy-fifth floor Kit is known as "Swiss Miss." She's become her master's eye, and she doesn't even know it.

They've changed the code to match another kind of process that doesn't need your voice. They figured out a way to jam ten thousand messages into one show, where previously they only had one per show. Your voice and face remained impenetrable for fifteen years, but they're afraid now it's being cracked.

CRICKETT: Cracked? I thought I was acting. I thought I was doing entertainment. I thought I had a career; but I'm working in a puppet factory, a Bat Cave, a Gong Show.

BALLOU: It has to be scanned fifty thousand times to come to the first level, then another million times to get to the next level, in a constantly revolving arbitrary code.

CRICKETT: Gobbledigook, kerfuffle afterkerfuffle. Does Heather Locklear know about this?!

20.

In the studio CRICKETT *shoots a scene from the remake of the film* Mildred Pierce, *starring* CRICKETT *as* MILDRED. *The actor playing* LEE *plays* MONTE. *The text of this scene should be the text from the original film. In this scene* MILDRED *confronts her lover* MONTE *and tells him to stay away from her daughter Veda. The scene ends with their breakup.* MILDRED *gives* MONTE *a check to finalize it. The last line is* MONTE'*s: "Mark our account paid in full."*

21.

KIT *is alone in* CRICKETT'*s dressing room trying on her kimono and looking at herself in the mirror.*

CRICKETT *enters.*

CRICKETT: What are you doing in my dressing room?

KIT: Nothing.

CRICKETT: What do you mean, nothing? What are you doing with my kimono?

KIT: Nothing.

CRICKETT: Why are you wearing my kimono?

KIT: I'm just looking at it.

CRICKETT: Why are you just looking at it?

KIT: I just like it.

CRICKETT: Well, it doesn't suit you. Take it off.

KIT: You don't think so?

CRICKETT: How did you get in here?

KIT: The intern let me in.

CRICKETT: Why did he do that?

KIT: I thought I forgot something in here.

CRICKETT: I don't like that intern.

KIT: What do you mean, you don't like him? It was your idea to hire him.

CRICKETT: I don't want him around—he's weird, I tell you. Fire him.

KIT: I can't—he's too valuable.

CRICKETT: How could he be valuable? He doesn't do anything but wander around and let people into my dressing room.

KIT: He's being prepped for a job upstairs. What's the matter with him?

CRICKETT: He has the strange ability to turn color into black-and-white. He appears out of nowhere and disappears into nowhere. He's always hovering around. He seems to see and know everything for no reason.

KIT: Let's not get into that tri-polar conversation again.

CRICKETT: What are you implying?

KIT: I'm implying that you are loosing it.

CRICKETT: He's a creep.

KIT: You used to be so smart, and now you're getting all fuzzy around the edges. Pick yourself up and stop freaking out at every little thing.

CRICKETT: Fire him.

KIT: No.

CRICKETT: He's getting into my head.

KIT: He's polite, isn't he?

CRICKETT: Yes. He's gentle and kind and charming, isn't he?

KIT: Yes.

CRICKETT: Baloney!

KIT: He runs lines with you when you ask him to, doesn't he?

CRICKETT: Yes, and then he changes the lines, and I don't remember them anymore.

KIT: He's supposed to deliver all the new script changes as soon as they come in.

CRICKETT: He's confusing me.

KIT: He's here to help you.

CRICKETT: To help me flip out. We have these strange conversations. He looks at me funny. Like he wants to make some kind of contact with me.

KIT: So don't talk to him and don't look at him. He's been a great help to us, so he'll have to stay, and you'll have to take a vacation.

CRICKETT: He's obliterating me.

KIT: Vacation.

22.

A scene from CRICKETT's latest miniseries. The CZARINA and her confidante, the COUNTESS CONCHITA, in the palace. CRICKETT as CONCHITA and the actress who plays KIT as the CZARINA. Prerecorded.

CRICKETT:—had to ... for political reasons, Czarina.

CZARINA: You were never very political, Conchita.

CRICKETT: Well ... I mean for spiritual reasons.

CZARINA: You were never very spiritual either.

CRICKETT: I know, but I've had a transformation ... through Rasputin.

CZARINA: I thought you hated him.

CRICKETT: I've had a change.

CZARINA: I myself thought I had been transformed also, but I know now that he is destroying the whole court through his charms. How could this have happened?

CRICKETT: I've found my inner soul.

CZARINA: And what is that soul made out of?

CRICKETT: Light.

CZARINA: It's made out of rotting garlic. I can smell it ... I told you never to talk to him.

CRICKETT: He is the one who will save this country from the likes of us. I truly believe it.

CZARINA: How can you? He's a terrifying presence, and now I can't rid myself of him. He's too powerful. Is this a bad dream, Conchita?

CRICKETT: No, my dear Czarina.

CZARINA: The entire court has become Rasputinized because of him. A Pimper's Paradise.

CRICKETT: Please be careful. Everything will soon be taken away from you.

CZARINA: When will it happen?

CRICKETT: It's already happening. It's already happened.

CZARINA: And my baby, the Czarino?

CRICKETT: Exquisitely ectomorphed away by a plasmatic cloud of splendiferous hemophilia.

CZARINA: Poor thing! How will it all end, Conchita?

CRICKETT: I can't say.

CZARINA: You can't—or won't?

CRICKETT: I can't because I won't; I won't because I can't.

CZARINA: It's my own fault. I never should have let Rasputin in here with his rumba band. He had his way with me when I thought I was having my way with him, and now he will have his way with all of us.

CRICKETT: And now it's too late—everyone is dancing the night away.

CZARINA: Midnight in Moscow. What will we do?

CRICKETT: Not much we can do. The sky is falling. I only wanted to warn you.

CZARINA: Why are you warning me if it's too late?

CRICKETT: Perhaps you can save yourself.

CZARINA: And my sister, Madame Karenina?

CRICKETT: Already gone, railroaded because of her blinding love for trains.

CZARINA: My little Anastasia?

CRICKETT: Anaesthetized in a seventy-year coma of ignorant bliss. There is nothing you can do.

CZARINA: And you? What will happen to you?

CRICKETT: I will stay ... and rule.

CZARINA: Traitor! My palace has become a rat's nest, and you, the Countess Rodentia. Book me a flight to Havana!

CRICKETT: You'll never escape.

CZARINA: You'll never escape.

CRICKETT: I have escaped.

CZARINA: I'll have your head.

CRICKETT: We have yours, no one needs mine. There will be no perestroika in the palace tonight.

CZARINA: I want you and Rasputin out of my palace.

CRICKETT: It's too late—he's slept with every lady-in-waiting in the palace.

CZARINA: How could they have slept with that greasy thing?

CRICKETT: Are you kidding? They couldn't wait .Why do you think they call them ladies-in-waiting?

CZARINA: Get him and his horny harem out of here!

CRICKETT: He's turned them all into bulging blintzes ready to unleash a billion-headed blintzkrieg of raging Rasputinos into the very heart of the Kremlin. Any day now, it shall be released. The end is near. The in-filtration is imminent.

CZARINA: Pack my suitcase. I'm going to Cleveland!

CRICKETT: Pack it yourself, Cleopatra!

CZARINA: Jezebel, Tokyo Rose, Rasputina!

CRICKETT: You've fallen asleep and forgotten to blow out the candle.

CZARINA: And me, what will happen to me?

CRICKETT: "I knew a girl who tried to walk across the lake. Of course it was winter and all this was ice. It's a hell of a thing to do, you know. They say the lake is as big as the ocean. I wonder if she knew about it? ..."*

Flames flash across screen.

---

* From "Walking on Thin Ice," by Yoko Ono.

23.

CRICKETT, asleep on her sofa, wakes up to ringing phone. She picks it up.

BALLOU: *(On phone.)* You're late for the shoot!

CRICKETT: The firing squad?!

BALLOU: The wedding of Nicholas and Alexandra! We were supposed to start taping an hour ago. Where have you been?!

CRICKETT: I must have fallen asleep. I ate a blintz the size of the Hindenburg last night. Conchita made it for me. I was trying to get into the part.

BALLOU: Get over here, the whole crew is waiting …

24.

CRICKETT, LEE, and KIT in KIT's office.

KIT: … We're having a little trouble with your interpretation of some of the lines.

CRICKETT: My interpretation?

LEE: You're invisible, transparent—we can see right through you.

CRICKETT: Isn't that what you always wanted from me—transparency?

KIT: Yes, but now it's too much. You haven't hidden yourself well enough.

CRICKETT: I hide myself perfectly inside every character you give me.

LEE: It's not enough. You haven't hidden yourself inside yourself well enough, and that is what is necessary here.

KIT: You're slipping. You're putting too much emphasis on how you say things. It's throwing the rhythm off. Sometimes it looks like you actually believe what you're saying. That you really know what you're talking about.

CRICKETT: With these scripts? That'll be the day.

LEE: And we don't mind so much, but other people do. You feel things too violently and deeply, and so—

CRICKETT: So what? It's hard enough working without a director. And all those geeks constantly taking notes.

LEE: You know we never use directors. We don't need them. They just confuse things. The coordinators and writers take care of everything. You've been here long enough to know that these things direct themselves.

KIT: As long as everyone involved doesn't get too involved.

CRICKETT: I've always done whatever you asked.

LEE: Always.

KIT: But truthfully, you've become a freak.

LEE: A Halloween mask.

KIT: Casper the friendly ghost.

CRICKETT: Boo!

KIT: You've moved past that natural mediocrity … You've gotten too good for your own good.

CRICKETT: How would you know the difference?

KIT: I was an actress once, too, you know.

CRICKETT: You thought you were. I never did.

LEE: Then think of it from the audience's point of view. You don't know what it's like having to watch you year after year.

CRICKETT: You don't know what it's like. To be driven like a camel up the hill and down the hill day by day. A little pack mule dragging your shit along the cliff side trying not to slip off. And I am very good at it.

KIT: But not so much anymore. You're starting to slip and stumble off the path. Get off it before you get pushed off.

CRICKETT: It's that weird intern, isn't it? He's been spying on me. What did he tell you?

LEE: It's not the intern; it's the endless list of weekly brain-battering miniseries you've memorized backwards and forwards and forwards and backwards. The wave after wave of desolate desolation you send out on your face night after night.

KIT: Now go and rearrange your face and get another job—or don't get one; you don't need one.

LEE: Get another life; or just get a life.

KIT: You've been everything; now you can be anything. Or at least pretend to be.

LEE: We're all pack mules delivering the message. Shows and actors come and go, but the message forever stays and must be sent. It's not the singer; it's the song.

CRICKETT: You've turned me into some kind of electronic airbag—a red hot chili pepper—and I didn't even know it. Going through my motions like an idiot puppet head. What an awful way to live. Emotion mining in the school of black memories.

LEE: Don't be so dramatic.

KIT: Now where were we? You have one year left of your contract. Five more shows. It won't be renewed. You've gotten away with murder, and now it's murder time, so be grateful to get away without spilling a drop of blood in the blood bath.

CRICKETT: What's happening here?

LEE: Nothing is happening here.

KIT: Something is happening here, and you don't know what it is, do you, Mister Jones?

LEE: Stay away from that intern.

CRICKETT: Why?

KIT: I knew a girl who tried to walk across a lake. Of course, it was winter and all this was ice. It's a terrible thing to do you know.

LEE: They say the lake is as big as the ocean.

KIT: I wonder if she knew about it.?

LEE: Farewell, my concubine.

CRICKETT: Hiroshima, *mon amour*.

25.

CRICKETT and BALLOU by her pool.

CRICKETT: … And they are mediocre and stupid.

BALLOU: But you do them anyway.

CRICKETT: I do.

BALLOU: They are mediocre and stupid, and you are mediocre, but you aren't stupid.

CRICKETT: But you write them anyway.

BALLOU: I do.

CRICKETT: Why? How can you stand writing all those coded scripts? Don't you feel like a hack? We must be making it for some reason. It must have some value.

BALLOU: The stuff is junk and everyone knows it; but I adapt their code to mine. They think I'm adapting myself to their code; but it's the other way around. I've imbedded my code into theirs, so I'm really writing what I want to. Their code is secondary to mine. As long as I understand it, what does it matter if anyone else does?

CRICKETT: Who is that code going to?

BALLOU: Myself.

CRICKETT: Where?

BALLOU: Messages between the hereafter and the thereafter.

CRICKETT: Oh, please don't tell me you see dead people! I couldn't bear it.

BALLOU: No way.

CRICKETT: What about everyone else?

BALLOU: What about them?

CRICKETT: What are you writing?

BALLOU: That western was really a novel.

CRICKETT: What was my part?

BALLOU: You were the narrator.

CRICKETT: I thought you hated narrators.

BALLOU: You are a narrator that breaks the narrator's code of conduct and alters the story. I'll give you the key to the code; then you'll know what you're really saying. It's like speaking another language that no one understands. I'm actually saying something else entirely.

CRICKETT: Don't you want anyone to understand it?

BALLOU: The beauty is in keeping it private. Especially here. I live in my own private city. That way everyone around me is blind, but I can see something they can't.

CRICKETT: Why are you blind?

BALLOU: I thought you'd never ask. I was born that way. It's a kind of mask.

CRICKETT: When I studied acting we learned that everyone carries three masks. The first one conceals you from the world in general. The second one conceals you from other people. The third one conceals you from yourself.

BALLOU: That old story. There are really four masks. The fourth one hides you from the other three, so that one is unaware of the masks altogether. I'm blind, so I get to have a fifth mask. Number five mask protects me from seeing anyone seeing me. It makes the other four masks irrelevant. I was born naked, and that's the way I stay. A world without clothes.

CRICKETT: What a relief. How many masks do you think I have?

BALLOU: Fifty or sixty. You're deep in mask country.

CRICKETT: It's the only country I know.

BALLOU: Find yourself another country.

CRICKETT: How?

BALLOU: One day we'll have a big bonfire and burn them all. Got a match?

26.

KIT and INTERN in KIT's office.

KIT: What are you doing in here? I thought you were running lines with Crickett.

INTERN: She fell asleep.

KIT: Then wake her up.

INTERN: She locked herself in her dressing room.

KIT: Here's the key. Open the door and wake her up—she has to get those lines down by tonight. And bring the key back.

INTERN: What are you doing?

KIT: What do you mean, what am I doing? I'm working.

INTERN: On what?

KIT: None of your business. You wouldn't understand.

INTERN: Yes I would.

KIT: Are you going to get me my coffee? I asked for it an hour ago.

INTERN: Did you?

KIT: I sure did. Go on and wake her up and get me my coffee.

INTERN: I just wanted to know what you were working on.

KIT: It's very complicated

INTERN: I know.

KIT: No you don't.

INTERN: Why did Cricket get killed in that show last night? It wasn't in the script.

KIT: Sometimes there are changes; the scriptwriters are very artistic and temperamental here.

INTERN: They don't seem to be.

KIT: How would you know?

INTERN: I was talking to them.

KIT: You have to leave them alone and let them work.

INTERN: They're stoned half the time. So are you.

KIT: I beg your pardon? I got you this job. What were you doing in here last night?

INTERN: What?

KIT: In my office.

INTERN: I wasn't in here.

KIT: Yes, you were videotaped—I reviewed it this morning.

INTERN: I was looking for something.

KIT: And what was that?

INTERN: I left a script in here.

KIT: I didn't see it. I have you on tape looking through my desk. What were you looking for?

INTERN: The script.

KIT: How did you get into the desk anyway—it was locked.

INTERN: No it wasn't.

KIT: My drawer is electronically locked at the end of the day. I also noticed you tried to get into my computer.

INTERN: But it was shut down and I couldn't get in.

KIT: What were you looking for?

INTERN: You don't want to know.

KIT: Yes I do.

INTERN: I could have you fired for this.

KIT: I could have you fired.

INTERN: Could you?

KIT: You know, we're being taped now.

INTERN: Yes.

KIT: Doesn't it bother you?

INTERN: No. Does it bother you?

KIT: No.

INTERN: It should. I need to look at your files, please.

KIT: Go ahead.

INTERN: Thank you. Could you leave for about an hour while I take care of some business?

KIT: Who are you working for?

INTERN: Who are you working for?

KIT: Supposedly we're working for the same company. You're freaking me out.

INTERN: I'm sorry about that.

KIT: What do you want?

INTERN: Just let me look at some files.

KIT: All right, I don't have anything to hide. How's your mother?

INTERN: Your sister? Why don't you call her and find out? Go and call her now.

KIT: I'm sure she'd like to know that you're sneaking into my office at night. It's a terrible thing to do, you know.

INTERN: She knows.

KIT: How old are you now?

INTERN: Seventeen.

KIT: Why do you bother Crickett so much?

INTERN: I don't.

KIT: Stay away from her.

INTERN: She docsn't miind.

KIT: Yes she does.

INTERN: Go and get yourself a cup of coffee and let me work.

KIT: What is this about? Shall we have dinner tonight and you can tell me?

INTERN: I'm not hungry.

KIT: You seem very hungry for something.

INTERN: It's not important.

KIT: It's not?

INTERN: Not really. Get out of here, will you?

KIT: What are you doing with my files? What did I do wrong?

INTERN: Will you get out of here and let me work?!

KIT: I'm just trying to save my ass.

INTERN: Free your mind, your ass will follow.

KIT: You were always a bizarre little child.

INTERN: Rasputina!

27.

On the set of a scene in a hospital room. CRICKETT is in the hospital bed. LEE,
BALLOU, and KIT are in the control room.

LEE: Okay, action.

CRICKETT remains motionless, eyes closed.

LEE: Crickett, we're rolling.

BALLOU: Crickett, are you okay? … Crickett, say something.

LEE: Cut. What is the matter with you?

BALLOU: Crickett?

Lee enters and shakes CRICKETT, but no response.

INTERN: Crickett? Can you hear me?

LEE: What's the matter with her?

BALLOU: She can't hear us. She doesn't know where she is.

LEE: Crickett, wake up. Start rolling.

BALLOU: Why?

LEE: Why not? We have to get something.

BALLOU: How long do we have to finish this thing?

LEE: Another week. We're behind schedule as it is. Just keep rolling and improvise.

INTERN: Shall we call an ambulance?

BALLOU: Call Dr. Dre.

28.

LEE and KIT argue in the hallway.

LEE: I told you, I can't take this anymore.

KIT: If I can, you can.

LEE: If you can, you can. I don't want to.

KIT: You can't leave now. You're responsible for this mess.

LEE: I shot the sheriff, but I didn't shoot no deputy.

KIT: You are the deputy.

LEE: Then shoot me. But I want out.

KIT: Oh, get a hold, get a grip. What's the big deal, we ship her off to a hospital. What do we have to do with her breakdown?

LEE: What about my breakdown?

KIT: Don't you break down on me, don't you go ape-shit on me now!

LEE: Don't get so dramatic.

KIT: The bottom is falling out, the sky is falling.

LEE: Get it together, will you? You're such a wimp. You always were.

KIT: I'm getting out before the shit hits the fan.

LEE: The shit has hit, and you have to stay here.

KIT: What time is it?

LEE: Three a.m.

KIT: We've been here two days, and she's still the same.

LEE: She's a fucking zombie.

KIT: Poisoned with perfection—she always was.

LEE: She keeps trying to say something.

KIT: Inject her again. Where is that writer?

LEE: The word whore? He's asleep. He's been writing for two days straight.

KIT: Has he come up with anything?

LEE: He's rearranged the whole script according to the equations. He had to collaborate with the code geeks. They spent all night arguing. It's a mess. It sounds like Beckett.

KIT: It'll have to do.

LEE: Where is that fool intern? I told him to keep an eye on her.

KIT: I think he's a spy from another company.

LEE: Don't you get it yet? He's a spy from our own company. He's your nephew—you hired him. I've got to get out of here.

KIT: Don't worry, I've shut down the cameras in here.

LEE: Are you sure?

KIT: See? It's not seeing anything.

LEE: It sees everything whether it's on or not.

KIT: Don't rock the boat.

LEE: Oh shut up, you stupid bitch. I am so sick of you and your pronouncements and orders!

KIT: If you're trying to get fired, it won't work.

LEE: Come on, fire me.

KIT: You've flipped, Mildred. You're always so nervous.

LEE: What about Crickett? I thought she was your friend.

KIT: Now she's just a zombie. Get over it. Leave her locked in the studio. I'm going up to my office and get some sleep.

LEE: I'm going home.

KIT: You are going to stay in that studio with her tonight.

LEE: I did it last night, and I'm not going to baby-sit her again. It's creepy.

KIT: Have some more meth.

LEE: "Shelter me from the powder and the finger." I'm going home.

KIT: Then we'll just leave her with the intern. Where is he?

LEE: Wandering around. He has a toothache.

KIT: Is he retarded or something?

LEE: He's weird.

KIT: Get everyone out of here. Clear the joint.

LEE: Mike, come here. I want you to stay in the studio with Crickett tonight.

INTERN: I'm not staying in there alone with that zombie!

KIT: Yes you are. You're staying in there with her. Yes you are, it's your job!

29.

KIT and LEE in KIT's office.

KIT: Where's that writer? I keep calling him, and he doesn't answer.

LEE: I gave him some sleeping pills, and I chained him to her bed. They're having a zombie script conference.

KIT: That won't work well with all the speed I gave him this morning.

LEE: This is getting sick. It's not so funny anymore.

KIT: When was it ever, Mildred?

LEE: Stop calling me Mildred.

KIT: You've totally whacked him out. You've corrupted him.

LEE: He was corrupt the minute he walked in here. Crickett's ex keeps calling for the alimony payments.

KIT: Then send him a check, Mildred.

LEE: If I'm Mildred Pierce, then you're Johnny Rotten.

They kiss violently and fall onto the desk to the Neil Young guitar riff from "Rust Never Sleeps." They separate suddenly.

KIT: But really, what's the matter with her?

LEE: She's suffering for her private thoughts of rebellion and doubt.

30.

Later that night. Studio. CRICKETT is knocked out in the bed on hospital set. BALLOU is asleep, chained to the bed with his laptop.

CRICKETT: *(Voice over.)* They seem to think I'm in some sort of a cloud coma. Even the doctor can't figure it out. But actually, I've mentally brought down a cloud upon myself. Shut myself down till I can figure this out. It's no big deal. I taught myself to do this as a child. It's a self-induced gag order. I just slow my body functions way down till it looks like I've checked out. Comatose. Incommunicado. But now I seem to be under some kind of house arrest for my insubordination—my quadrophenia—till they figure out what to do with me. But I'm not going to finish that crappy script. I'll just stay this way till they give up. Oh Jesus, I forgot to send the alimony payment. I'll try to make some motions so that they send the check out. Hey, Ballou! Where is that stupid intern? Over here! ... Hey!!

CRICKETT makes crude motions of signing a check. LEE and KIT enter.

KIT: What did she say?

BALLOU: She wants us to send the alimony check.

KIT: Now she's out again.

LEE: No she's not. Wake up, Crickett! Say something ...

KIT: Listen, honey, you had better come out of this right now and start behaving. Are you going to, or not?

CRICKETT: Not.

LEE: I'll tell everyone you're a crack-head.

KIT: We'll arrange a nice autopsy for you.

CRICKETT: *(Garbled.)* Fuck you.

LEE: What? What did she say?

BALLOU: I think she said "fuck you."

LEE: We're going to lose our biggest client. I knew we shouldn't have given her this part.

CRICKETT: *(Garbled.)* Cash cow.

KIT: What?

CRICKETT: Rasputina!

LEE: Call the doctor and inject her with something.

INTERN: He couldn't find a vein. They've shrunken into undetectability.

KIT: Ballou, wake up! Get online with the programmers and see if you can work out a story line where she dies in the hospital bed.

BALLOU: That's not how the story goes. We're only halfway through the plot, and we can't kill her off—she's the star of the show.

LEE: Then change it. I want her killed or dead before we start shooting tomorrow morning.

INTERN: That's in six hours, you moron.

KIT: Just kill her off, and we can figure out the rest this week. Talk to the code people and see if you can work the daughter in as the main character.

CRICKETT: You're going to give that horrible actress the starring role?

LEE: What?

CRICKETT: *(Garbled sounds.)*

KIT: What did you say?

CRICKETT: *(Garbled sounds.)*

LEE: This is your last show here, sister. You are so out of here.

KIT: Her character is dying anyway—just shoot around it.

BALLOU: Crickett's character doesn't die. Her cousin does, and she doesn't die till the end of the script, and we're in the middle.

LEE: Then shoot the end.

BALLOU: Her cousin doesn't die in a hospital; she dies in a Ferris wheel accident.

KIT: So what! Crickett's character is dying in this show right now in the middle of the story. Make something up with the geeks.

LEE: Can we get her to close her eyes?

BALLOU: No.

LEE: We need them closed for the death scene.

KIT: People can die with their eyes open, too, you know.

LEE: Okay, all right! Leave it like that.

BALLOU: But we need Crickett's voice, or it won't code right.

LEE: Well, get some pieces of her voice and mix it so it's her voice over it. Just splice around it

KIT: How long will that take?

BALLOU: A few hours with the computer. She can narrate.

LEE: How is she supposed to be narrating if she's dying?

KIT: Just do it!

LEE: What a stupid story then.

KIT: It's stupid anyway.

31.

BALLOU, KIT, and LEE in control room. BALLOU typing.

LEE: ... To what?

KIT: How the hell would I know? I just got a call from upstairs.

LEE: The show has already hit the feed—it's broadcasting according to plan. Pull it.

KIT: We can't. It's been requested that we change the message midstream. Call in the master geeks and get them online with Ballou. They've got to concoct something new. The message has to be changed before the show completes its broadcast.

LEE: It's twenty minutes into the feed. It runs for another hour and ten minutes.

KIT: It has to be reedited while it's running.

LEE: We can't change the code and reedit it in that time.

KIT: We have to. Where is Crickett?

LEE: She's knocked out on the hospital set. She won't come out of her zombie funk. But we did find out a way to kill off her character.

KIT: Get her to Studio D and tell her to stand by. Where is the contingency itinerary? We have to change the whole plot.

BALLOU: I can't think of another plotline that fast.

KIT: Start writing. Send it straight to the teleprompter. We'll reedit it and cut it into the broadcast live.

BALLOU: Where are we?

LEE: Minute twenty-five—she's throwing a birthday party for her father.

KIT: Here are the requirements. Change it.

LEE: Ballou, what do you have for us?

BALLOU: Party's over. It's a funeral now.

LEE: There's a funeral scene in next week's show—remove it and lay it in at the beginning of the intro after the next commercial. Paint her party dress black on the computer.

32.

LEE goes to studio to wake up CRICKETT.

LEE: Crickett dear… honey …

CRICKETT: *(Drowsy.)* What?!

LEE: Come on, get up, you have work to do!

CRICKETT: What?

LEE: Get moving, sister, your sleeping beauty act is over. Go over to wardrobe and makeup with the intern. Get her a quadruple espresso with a shot of Karmalatte.

CRICKETT: Why? What time is it?

LEE: TIME TO ACT.

33.

CRICKETT is dragged in front of a camera.

CRICKETT: … What are you talking about? We finished shooting that last week. Isn't it broadcasting tonight?

LEE: We have to do it again. Shut up and read.

CRICKETT: But I don't know what I'm saying.

LEE: Yes you do. Just talk.

CRICKETT: Well who am I? What's happening?

KIT: We have five minutes before this section ends.

LEE: Then what?

KIT: Then go into the outtake file, and pull her reaction shots, and lay some digital tears on her face.

LEE: But she's laughing here.

KIT: Add a lot of tears and they won't know the difference. Tell her to narrate this new monologue about the funeral.

CRICKETT: (Reading from the teleprompter.) … I was so happy, and then my happiness turned to tears as I realized that in fact it was not a party but a funeral. I didn't know whether to laugh or cry, so I did both.

KIT: Are these words qualified for the new script?

LEE: Are you sure?

BALLOU: Yes, they've all been adapted to the new code.

KIT: Are you sure?

BALLOU: Geek three has justified and reordered them.

LEE: All right. We're up to minute twenty-five and we're doing fine—the message is conforming.

KIT: What about the word "tears?"

BALLOU: Yes, it fits into the pattern.

LEE: Take another speedball.

BALLOU: I just took three, and if I take anymore I'm gong to blow a synapse. Leave me alone!

LEE: I'm just trying to help.

BALLOU: Then shut up and feed me the coordinates.

INTERN:

Ddj348578d9dddkvvnddfhd///.,dld;ew'doddjvnfedadbvbizvnsi385500(*&^

BALLOU: Is that backslash correct?

LEE: Yes.

KIT: Check it again. Is it correct?

BALLOU: Oh shit, no, it's not.

KIT: Then what is it?

LEE: It's a dot.

BALLOU: Then I've got to lengthen her monologue by twelve seconds. "I looked at the swans on the lake and became morose and pale and … and …

CRICKETT: I looked at the swans on the lake and became morose and pale and … and … and what?!

KIT: Tell her to slow it down.

LEE: Slow it down.

BALLOU: And we need another word with an 'm' at the beginning.

KIT: Muffins.

LEE: Does it fit?

BALLOU: Yes, okay, muffins.

CRICKETT: That doesn't make any sense.

BALLOU: So what.

KIT: Too late now. It's being dubbed over the crying scene and the outtakes from the swan parade.

CRICKETT: I hated that scene.

LEE: It's in. We have to use it. The swans fit the code.

BALLOU: I hate swans.

KIT: Shut up.

LEE: Take the car accident and lay it into the Indy 500 race we never used last year.

BALLOU: What?

LEE: Do it.

KIT: Put her in the stands and tell her to start reading the next line.

BALLOU: Who is she talking to?

KIT: Her sister.

BALLOU: Her sister is supposed to be in Tucson, Arizona.

CRICKETT: Get back, JoJo!

KIT: Then give her a cell phone. Tell her to talk into it.

LEE: Talk into the cell phone, Crickett. Read, Crickett, read.

CRICKETT: Hello, dear, how are you? No, I can't go to rehab again. There's nothing wrong with me ... How is the dog? I'll be coming home in a few weeks, so take care of her. The muffins were beautiful at the funeral.

LEE: We're ten minutes ahead.

BALLOU: How much left?

KIT: We have to conform the rest of it over the next hour, change the shirt her husband's wearing to blue. Can you give him a mustache?

BALLOU: I know he didn't have a mustache ten minutes ago, but so what.

KIT: The last ten minutes of the show are the most crucial. We have to cram it all in at the end, so start thinking.

BALLOU: I can't think that fast. The funeral car race, swans, then she—... Well, by the coordinates, we have to have her turn into an alcoholic.

CRICKETT: She's already an alcoholic.

LEE: Give her a drink.

KIT: Anything—just keep drinking, Crickett.

BALLOU: She has to be drinking a rum and Coke.

LEE: Just color the glass.

KIT: Doesn't make sense.

BALLOU: Then we have to change the end … She doesn't marry the count but she—

INTERN: She jumps into the river.

BALLOU: Hey, that's good—that will work.

LEE: Will you shut up? You're just an intern.

BALLOU: So far he's had the best suggestions. Keep talking, Mike.

LEE: You're going to let the intern write this?

BALLOU: Yes, if I have to. I can't think that fast. I need help—my imagination is under attack. Mike, what else?

INTERN: Then she goes underwater.

BALLOU: Yes, that's good—swimming pool—that fits perfectly. Is that right, geek three? … Yes? Okay, she's in a swimming pool.

KIT: She just jumped into a river.

LEE: Fold the river into a swimming pool; then she's underwater.

BALLOU: And comes up to breathe, and survives, and has a transformation, and becomes sober.

KIT: Then get her to read this monologue over the pool scene. Just plug this straight into the teleprompter.

LEE: Crickett, start reading into the camera.

BALLOU: Don't look at the screen, you'll only get disgusted.

CRICKETT: I realized after my near drowning in the pool that I would survive being dunked into the drink and that I never would take another drink. I found my soul in that pool. My soul was made out of light as I traveled toward the air above me and the sky and the sun and the light … There is another world, a better world for me … Are you serious? Someone get me a drink!!

LEE: Okay, that's it. We have three minutes left of empty time.

KIT: Put the swans on, and make sure they're encoded not to mean anything. Devoid them and lay them in under the credits. Change the names on the credits to these names. I've worked them out to conform.

LEE: But none of these names are even in the show.

BALLOU: I made up the names to finish out the message in code. I couldn't think of anymore lines.

KIT: Just lay them in—they have to end by the last four seconds. And then four seconds of pure, deep, constricted black. And it's done.

34.

The studio hallway. A few days later.

INTERN: Well, how did it go?

LEE: The show was a bomb.

INTERN: The show, or the show?

LEE: Both.

KIT: Slammed silly, the worst reviews you ever saw; but great reviews for Crickett. They say she'll get a special Emmy for it …

LEE: The Golden Glob.

INTERN: Your acting has been described as a "combination of alcoholic mania, pure terror, and a triumph of the human spirit."

CRICKETT: How could that be? I didn't even know what I was saying.

KIT: It won't be the first time you've gotten an Emmy for that.

LEE: The best portrayal of mania since Greta Garbo.

KIT: Jean-Luc Godard just called.

CRICKETT: Who's that?

35.

INTERN and LEE in LEE's office.

LEE: … Who?

INTERN: The geeks, the senior writers, the producers. Each in their own department working separately from each other on different functions that are combined at the crucial moment.

LEE: I thought those geeks were just a bunch of hippie hop-heads.

INTERN: Half of them are mainlining Ecstasy on a daily basis to keep up with the demand.

LEE: Including your aunt?

INTERN: She's been in a K-hole since '88. And performing admirably under the circumstances.

LEE: How would you know that?

INTERN: She has a website too—we all do. All these secret websites are interactive. They share information with each other like a living, breathing organism. It keeps a balance within the entity. Organically, automatically, second by second. Sometimes there's an imbalance, and someone has to drop out.

LEE: Like that queen in management?

INTERN: His name was Jeremy.

LEE: He shot himself at Chang's Mongolian Grill, didn't he?

INTERN: You think he did, but that is definitely contraindicated. He was assassinated.

LEE: *(Laughing.)* By whom?

INTERN: Oh, just some jerk. I think they paid a homeless schizophrenic to do it.

LEE: Who paid him?

INTERN: It was dictated by the website override.

LEE: Override?

INTERN: When there is an imbalance that can't be internally corrected it's indicated on the mainframe, and a directive is made for the outcome. Then it's just a matter of hours before it's completed and the system goes back into harmony. The websites have all been taught to compete automatically for survival while searching for the harmonic options that are the main objective.

LEE: Harmony?

INTERN: Except that Jeremy released information to me. Which I passed on to Ballou. But now he has become imbalanced and has begun to suffer. The sensors are indicating it on his website.

LEE: How do you know all this?

INTERN: I'm not stupid, you know.

36.

LEE and CRICKETT at CRICKETT's house.

CRICKETT: ... What do you mean, I'm a website?

LEE: Crickett, I'm sorry to tell you this, but they've constructed a secret million-page website around you over fifteen years, with every piece of information about you that you can imagine.

CRICKETT: But how?

LEE: From the television shows, footage from your house and dressing room, medical information, biological impulses, every telephone call you've made for the last twenty years. They started research on you long before they hired you.

CRICKETT: What for?

LEE: They test out codes against your vital physical and psychological information—it helps them figure out ideas for plots and possible variations on message formations. You probably have the world's largest and most comprehensive website.—This coffee is awful, by the way.—For years it was a goldmine, an endless fountain of the most beautiful and complex equations. But now it's become useless. As you aged over the last fifteen years, every weight fluctuation, facial inflection, voice change was tracked and used to create newer and more complicated codes. Entire shows were built around that nose job you had last year. How could this have happened?

CRICKETT: You knew they bugged my house and dressing room, and you never told me. That's how it happened, you stupid dumb fuck!

LEE: I thought they were just checking up on you. All the offices have been bugged for years. We knew about the crypto stuff, but not about the websites.

CRICKETT: How do you know all this?

LEE: The intern told me.

37.

INTERN and KIT at KIT's house.

KIT: Can't you see you're upsetting me?

INTERN: You all seem to suffer so much. Is it a generational thing?

KIT: You're still in high school—why are you asking me these things? Don't you want to be a kid?

INTERN: What's a kid anyway?

KIT: You're scaring me.

INTERN: I'm sorry.

KIT: You're bizarre. Get out of here, and forget about the coffee—it's probably poisoned.

INTERN: It is—on a daily basis.

KIT: With what?

INTERN: Different potions are delivered to different people. There are fifty-four prescriptions for this floor alone. You get a little bit of valium every day.

KIT: You've been eating too many double cheeseburgers.

INTERN: I don't eat meat

KIT: Then you're a bloodthirsty vegetarian, a vampire, and you're freaking me out.

INTERN: I didn't mean to. I just wanted to let you know what's going on.

KIT: It's too much to deal with.

INTERN: Then you should leave. You're on your way out anyway. Don't accept any invitations to Chang's Mongolian. Get out before you get pushed out.

KIT: Do you have a website?

INTERN: Yes. But I add conflicting information to it every day through the main computer. You should really leave now.

KIT: Why don't you just go work in a record store?

INTERN: I did. It was a bore.

KIT: Get out of here, please!

INTERN: Would you like some coffee?

KIT: Never again.

INTERN: Ballou should get out of here, too.

KIT: Who are you anyway?

INTERN: Your nephew. I've been sent to bring the house down.

KIT: And where will you end up when Babylon crumbles?

INTERN: I won't survive.

KIT: Why not?

INTERN: Kamikaze—the Divine Wind.

KIT: More like the Divine Miss Eminem.

INTERN: That little faggot? I hate that shit.

KIT: Who sent you?!

INTERN: I sent myself.

38.

CRICKETT and INTERN at CRICKETT's home.

CRICKETT: Well, what is it? Some kind of teenage suicide squad?

INTERN: I work alone. I was supposed to kill you, but I couldn't bear to do it. I love your acting.

CRICKETT: You do?

INTERN: I've seen everything you've ever done. So I won't kill you. I don't want you to suffer. You suffer enough.

CRICKETT: Why all this killing? Why does everyone have to be killed?

INTERN: It's the way of the world.

CRICKETT: Says who?

INTERN: It's happening all around you. You get killed on a yearly basis.

CRICKETT: Yes, but it's my job. You don't have to kill everyone to fix this. Just get everyone fired, unplug the damn thing, and get on with your life. Who are you working for?

INTERN: Myself.

CRICKETT: Everyone works for someone whether they know it or not.

INTERN: Zombie is as zombie does.

CRICKETT: I wish everyone would stop calling me a zombie—I'm not the only one in this place.

39.

INTERN in CRICKETT's bedroom, three A.M. CRICKETT is asleep.

CRICKETT: *(Waking with a start.)* Jesus! What are you doing in my house? It's the middle of the night.

INTERN: You looked like you were having such a good sleep.

CRICKETT: I had a hideous dream about the baby Caligula, starring you.

INTERN: I have to go. The holy city is about to go under. The websites have begun to flip out and erase each other.

CRICKETT: No Kamikaze?

INTERN: I've lost my taste for Kamikaze. I'm going south.

CRICKETT: Will we meet again?

INTERN: I don't think so. But why should you believe me? I'm the narrator, and you can never trust a narrator. But I'm resigning my spot as narrator. I'm going to Memphis.

CRICKETT: Don't go. I have reason to believe we all will be deceived in Graceland.

INTERN: I'm going anyway. If you know what's good for you, you won't take over the narration. It's a messy job. You wouldn't like it.

CRICKETT: Someone has to do it.

INTERN: No one has to do it. The story is telling itself.

CRICKETT: I hope so.

INTERN: Get out before you get pushed out.

CRICKETT: I am. I've booked a flight to Havana.

INTERN: Will we meet again?

CRICKETT: I hope so.

INTERN: Can I have your autograph?

CRICKETT: Sure.

INTERN: Consider my account paid in full.

CRICKETT: Memphis, *mon amour.*

40.

KIT sitting in a dark movie theater eating popcorn and watching a film. Her voice over her image.

KIT: *(Voice over.)* My nephew has renounced his spot as the narrator, and thank God. But a seventeen-year-old should never be narrating anyway—how do you think we got into this mess? So I've had to take over. I fired him tonight. The poor boy left with the idea that he had set the system to erase itself and go up in smoke. He had this fantasy that as the narrator he could control the story. But he is sadly mistaken. He understood a lot about the studio. But he didn't understand the other half of human nausea. I'm nothing but a speed freak zombie, and zombie is as zombie does, so I must do what I must do. Because of their natural inclination to envy and pettiness, our websites have set to fighting amongst themselves for survival. Because Crickett's website was the largest and most sophisticated, it replicated itself many times over according to her many characters' qualities. The other websites have begun to refer to her as Sybil. Leave it to them to cast the perpetrator as a woman. I was on my way to Chang's Mongolian for what I'm sure was a poisoned lunch with some executives. But I asked the limo driver to stop and let me buy a pack of cigarettes. I ducked into a movie theater. It's showing one of Crickett's films. I've been here all afternoon. They know I've skipped out. I'm so hungry, and this popcorn is making me ill. I can't go home. I'll have to figure out where to go when it's over. I'm falling asleep. But I can't fall asleep. If I do, someone else will take over the narration, and then I'm lost for sure.

41.

LEE in his office. His voice over his image.

LEE: Poor Kit, she was in over her head. She never should have listened to her nephew, and neither should you. He's lying about everything.

INTERN: *(Voice over.)* What are you talking about? I was trying to help her.

LEE: This is your fault. Ever since you got here everything has gone wrong, you stupid dumb fuck. I'm narrating now, do you mind? Go away. Anyway, I thought everything was going fine until I discovered through the intern that for years we were all replicated in a parallel Web world. Now the company seems to be an afterthought—Sybil's afterthought. One of Crickett's aliases placed the directive to kill Jeremy at Chang's Mongolian. In its urge to survive, the Sybil consortium has issued a directive to remove Crickett—the source of its inspiration. As Crickett's website subsidiaries increased, they became jealous of her endless fountain of inspiration. As it came to life, it learned the first rule of living: Life is a cannibal—it eats itself. A hungry mob is a hungry mob. So what if I didn't know half of what was going on? A limo has been waiting outside for two days to take me to Chang's Mongolian, but I hate Chinese food for reasons you can understand. I'm starving, but I'm not going anywhere near that place. Kit won't answer my calls. Someone else is sitting at her desk now. Mike? Are you still there? I can't stand that kid. I'm still narrating, so I guess he's gone.

42.

INTERN's voice over various shots.

INTERN: That's what he thinks. All of this wasn't what I imagined it would be when I began my attempt to bring it down. It will come down, but my small cloud has become a hurricane. My aunt thought I didn't understand, but I do understand. I understand that she's tied to something that can't be untied—it only can be cut. She's in over her head, and so they will have her head. Ballou was going to come with me, but he stayed to finish the last chapter of his novel. Now, I'm walking along a road. I'm hitchhiking somewhere in Arizona. A limousine offered me a ride, but I said no and ran away. I'll get another ride soon. Crickett's website became a plague of locusts eating everything in sight … Now I'm in Virginia somewhere. Isn't that north of Memphis though? Last night I snuck into a theater and caught the last half of one of Crickett's films, *The Shattering Mist*—the one about the Holy City. Memphis was a holy city. I just had lunch at McDonald's. I used the last money I took from my aunt's purse, but I'm almost there. I have to give up this narrating. It's getting to be a bad habit. How can anything ever happen to me if I already know what's going to happen? Who am I talking to anyway? I'm tired of explaining everything anyway, so I will renounce it forever. So I'm signing off. See you in Memphis. You'll never hear my voice again.

43.

CRICKETT in an airplane seat. Two screens show BALLOU wandering around empty hallways and offices filled with smoke.

CRICKETT: Our narrator has apparently quit. Since I don't hear anyone else talking, I suppose I have to take over now. He should be halfway to Memphis. It was all I could do to stop my alias entities from killing him on the side of the road. Forty thousand headless horsemen couldn't have stopped me. I do have the right to believe that the last half of the movie will be better than the rest of the film. Here I am running away from my own website. And the cloud finally appeared, but not as I had expected. Or maybe I had remembered it incorrectly. When the files were erased, the thrashers exploded and let down a rain of shreds twenty miles square. It snowed here, where it hadn't snowed in a thousand years. I can see it from the plane window on my way to Havana. It's some kind of secret homage to the suffering of those of us who have been forced to create it—to our determined efforts to force anything we can out of nothing—and it ain't nothin' but a heartache—a pop secret with extra butter. All the faces I made, all the crocodile tears I cried. All the times I killed, all the times I died. Why did I do it? People could say I was greedy. It wasn't greed; it was hunger. In a famine they say let them eat dirt, and I did—and I passed the plate. Shared it. And my mouth is burning. But our bellies are full. It wasn't a holy city; it was a holy machine. Could I have another brandy, please? Would you like one, too, Conchita? We're sitting here like two peanuts in coach class. These were the only tickets available. When I left the studio disguised as an old Japanese woman, Ballou wouldn't come with me. I hope he escapes the cloud. For my last act as narrator I will tell you that he escapes, and in two weeks we hungrily devour a platter of rice and beans in Havana. From here on, the story has a right to move on against the will of the narrator, so I'm going to stop talking now. The people sitting next to us are getting nervous.

Fade to all screens showing smoke-filled offices.

Firefall

For Robin Ashley

Firefall premiered at Dance Theater Workshop February 4-7, 2009. *Firefall* was assisted in its development by the Franklin Furnace Fund, a Bessie Schönberg/First Light DTW commission, the 2006 Artist-in-Residence Program at Eugene Lang College/The New School for Liberal Arts, New York City, and the MacDowell Colony.

Cast

R: Rachel Bell
F: Claire Buckingham
JESUS: Ben Forster
K: Kyle Griffiths
MARY: Stephanie Silver
PEEWEE: Ray Roy
JESUS: Ben Forster

Ray Roy: *Technical Direction and Web System Design*
Jeff Nash: *Lighting*
Jennifer Ortega: *Assistant Director*

Directed and designed by John Jesurun

There are eight character/players, each with an initial directive:

R tries to preserve the status quo of the suggested presentation situation inside the theater.

MARY tries to subvert what is happening by introducing false/conflicting information to create a new order in which she believes. She attempts to change the perceived reality of what is happening in the world during the performance.

F tries to find a common ground between the introduction of chaos and the status quo.

ISCARIOT is in a constant state of doubt and changes sides as is convenient to his own interest, which is being on the winning side.

PEEWEE is merely a trickster and tries to introduce chaos exclusively for its own sake.

K is the dummy. He apparently has no idea what is going on.

NOSEWORTHY follows and executes the rules closely.

JESUS (on video).

Note on the text: *The central hub of the content and form of* Firefall *is its omnipresent Website. In itself it becomes a "character" to be dealt with—a kind of "author." All material connected to the project is added and stored on this Website. This includes the project's entire text, as well as notes on rehearsals, photos, tech info, index, video and music clips, links, trivia, etc. Each character/player has their own section to which they may add material. Other than live Internet streams, all pre-recorded material used during the performance is accessed live through this constantly changing Website.*

The seven performers, director, and tech all have live Internet connection to their own laptops during all rehearsals and performances. They are encouraged to use the Internet simultaneously with rehearsing/performing memorized material. They also can communicate with each other by computer during the rehearsal/performance, visually as well as in text. All laptops are fitted with Webcams. All Internet/computer activity is visible onscreen to the audience. There is one live camera on stage.

One performer is the designated "interrupter," or modifier, of live memorized scenes. He can attempt at will to interrupt the proceedings with a live Internet connection to a news event, or an item on the Firefall *site, etc., and stop or alter the scene. This interventional aspect of the process has great potential and will continue to be developed. Performers and author can continuously add material to the "character" sections. These "character" sections have the potential of spinning off into their own Websites. The constantly developing presence of the Website beyond any performance becomes the potential factor* FOR *the continuing development and tension of this open-ended form. The original text is the basis for a form that is growing in all directions. The text itself is open-ended and will expand and change as well.*

Stage: *A large horizontal screen above the actors. It has three sections. The live laptop images of each of the seven performers, as well as an eighth laptop of the director, are projected across the screen in changing formations. Large images of live* OR *pre-recorded faces of the performers also share the screen at times. Performers sit at a long table, each in front of a laptop that they use during the performance.*

MARY: *(Her face center screen.)* They only come around when things are bad. I thought she was trying to console me because of the terrible death of my child now referred to as "you know who." But I realized later she was trying to become some kind of … or she had secret wishes of … becoming a writer and was using me to observe my private and deliriously sad moments at a very close range. She hoped that by being so near me she could see it from the inside and then learn how to imitate it for her writing. She was hoping to recreate it somehow by observing it. That's what she thought art was—imitating private moments of disaster. And therefore she could be perceived as doing deep passionate work as a writer and thinker. So all the time I was crying, she was watching and pretending to console me. But she was just feeding the flames and watching, as more tears fell out of my face. My face was burning, and she was kindly adding more kindling. Instead of saying, "Pull back the tears from your eyes so you'll learn the hard way." But there is only the hard way. OR no way at all. Glory without sound. But it was the horrible sound of death on my face that she was inspecting the whole time—trying to understand it so she could see what it was really like, and then write about it in imitation of life. And be seen as deep. But she was always deep. Deeper than I was. But I don't believe that—but you do. The idea is to take someone and make something out of them. For yourself. Making something out of someone else's soul. That's why she ended up in the city government. Because that's where you do that sort of thing. But suffering came to her, and she didn't appreciate it. She turned away from it as much as she could. And then I couldn't help her.

MARY's *face onscreen is replaced by F.*

F: That way I wouldn't really have to suffer the job of revealing or making it out of my own soul—and I could remain intact. My soul would remain intact, and I would survive longer than the rest by not having to feel all that suffering first-hand. I had an aversion to it. I would survive longer. It was about surviving and avoiding the pain. Somehow I would come out ahead or better than, or get more for my money and be worth more as a person. She's really a Jew pretending not to be one. They of course know and let her pretend so they can hold something over her. And therefore make things go more smoothly for them. I went to that funeral not because I mourned for the lost soul of the man who didn't care for me. Because I didn't care for him either. I went to find out something. Something about emotion perhaps. Something that I lacked and for the life of me could not find, so I always faked it. At times I wondered if I was amoral. Like the Germans or the Japanese—bred into me. Or born with a psychopathic urge that sped along in my life force. Anyway ...

Onstage PEEWEE stands facing K sitting at other end of table.

PEEWEE: The importance is to create an upper selection to keep the lower vastly from getting any of their things. We realize now that in the selection of the elite it doesn't matter what color they are. Because they all can succumb to the pleasures of luxury and status and, like all humans and animals, they will not like to relinquish them under pain of death even. For they realize that, in holding it together for their friends, they can keep it and distribute it to their own benefit and specifications. And the ones selected will think they are so special, and better than their own roots and even their own parents. And will come in willingly and happily and do the bidding of the selectors to keep in their favor. They realize that the selectors may become displeased and threaten sending them back to the ghetto from which they will never return and be derided by their own people as being too uppity. If they are sent back, then they will be rejected by both sides—the worst fate of all. They are fighting for big stakes.

K: Sort of like being gay.

PEEWEE: Anyway, how would you like that to happen to you?

K: Oh, I wouldn't mind. Being gay now is quite an honor.

PEEWEE: Not for too much longer.

K: Its shelf life is just about up.

PEEWEE: Get that dog out of here! *(Holds his arm out, pointing.)*

K: You told me I could bring it.

PEEWEE: I said that you could bring a stuffed replica.

K: But I'll have to kill it.

PEEWEE: Exactly. It will only enter these halls if it is dead. Kill it and stuff it, or get it out of here.

K: Come here, Lucifer.

PEEWEE: No one names their dog Lucifer.

K: God did.

PEEWEE: And now look at the world. Get that friggin' maccaca out of here!

Both remain throughout following video, K sitting, PEEWEE pointing.

K: *(Face crying on center screen, pre-recorded.)* I must get rid of the dog. It has a beautiful kind of life, living in a brilliantly painted, constructed garden of fantasy which has its own imitations of reality to satisfy; but still stays intact and unchanged. Through its eye it is "like seeing a garden at night in which certain parts are lit up so brightly that we can distinguish each blade of grass, each minute insect, each nuance of color—while the rest of the garden and the tidal wave that threatens it remain in darkness."* That dog's one good eye is a form for constant reinterpretation. The world in which he judged everything harshly and made reality conform to the reality of his judgments—and bend to his will—and make and unmake possibilities—is now cut in half. And now at this age his use of that eye has come back to haunt him. He is a victim of his own preposterously vain attempt to control time and reality. And worst of all, the lives and futures of others. The only reason he did it was that he was not interested in pure melody, but in the controlling of it and those who make it. Like any good politician. I can't believe I'm saying this about a dog, but it's true.

PEEWEE and ISCARIOT look at MARY and sing the opening verses of Lou Reed's "Perfect Day" to Scala's choral version playing in background.

PEEWEE and ISCARIOT: "Oh, it's such a perfect day," etc.

ISCARIOT: *(To MARY.)* If I can sing this song perfectly, then I will be this song, even though I didn't write it. It will be me. I will be as powerful as the person who wrote it. I can be the song, and the song can be me.

---

* A comment by the author Ivan Morris on the Japanese memoir *Sarashina Nikki.*

When I sing, it will be the most beautiful thing in the world, the most beautiful sound in the world. Oh Peewee, I am bewildered. I don't even believe in what I just said. How can I make the most beautiful sound in the world? My mind refuses to believe in anything—it is made that way. I am made that way. How can I be a song I never wrote? I refuse to believe that I can be a song I never wrote by singing it so well. I refuse, rather than be fooled by the weakness of belief. It's a strength, not a weakness, to "not believe." I disbelieve strongly, but not passionately. But I believe dispassionately, acceptingly. To accept and be part of the harmonious harmony of acceptance. But I refuse to accept. My mind will not do it. It will not bend. But if it will bend, it will break. That is my fear, and fear weakens the soul. My mind refuses to believe in anything but the strength of itself and its own singularity.

F: Isn't that a bit lonely? What if others believe like you ... that their minds must be independent and singular? Then you yourself become part of their belief system. Will you then continue to be so singular now that you are also part of something? Knowing that others disbelieve as you do?

ISCARIOT: They don't. I believe and disbelieve alone. That is the comfort and power in it.

F: Comfort and power? Is that what you want?

ISCARIOT: *(To PEEWEE.)* Your breath smells.

F: Your mind smells. It's rotting in its singularity. No one has opened the door in a while to that Caligari Cabinet. It's become tarantulized.

ISCARIOT: You're typing with your eyes closed ...

F: Confidently.

ISCARIOT: On the wrong keys.

F: Undo.

ISCARIOT: Cats think that way.

F: Confidently.

ISCARIOT: Animals believe.

F: Why would an animal believe—and what would it believe in?

ISCARIOT: It believes that its master will bring it lunch every day.

F: I bring you yours.

ISCARIOT: It only works till the day the cat doesn't get lunch.

F: Then what?

ISCARIOT: He doesn't believe anymore.

F: And hates his master for it …

ISCARIOT: Who cares about the master?!

F: What about the animals in the jungle who don't get a free lunch?

ISCARIOT: He gets a free lunch because he believes.

F: Until he doesn't get it and stops believing.

ISCARIOT: And the ant in the jungle believes like all the other ants.

F: … in the hive.

ISCARIOT: Anthill thinking. I can't believe I'm having this conversation with a secretary.

F: A fellow ant. That should tell you how pointless it is. What do you want for lunch?

PEEWEE and ISCARIOT: *(Singing to MARY.)* "Oh, it's such a perfect day," etc.

K sits at table and plays electric guitar softly while NOSEWORTHY speaks.

NOSEWORTHY: *(Back to audience, he faces center camera and his image is projected on center screen.)* Yes, but it's a very intimate language. You wouldn't understand it. The shadowland is a place where people violently believe in something or everything because they have to, they need to. Keep an eye on Mary; she's like that. It's not like where we are, where no one has to believe in anything. We have the right not to believe in anything. We are free, so we don't have to. Who needs the pain? But you know that. (*K hits a few loud power chords; then returns to playing softly.*) They don't know how to suffer properly anyway. They suffer—but it's decorated suffering. You know, all buttered over—not too heavy, not too deep, if they can help it. But that's all right. They can't stand the very idea of it. But that's all right. The time will come again. There was a time in the history of humanity when people would get sick and die when someone didn't love them anymore, like animals. But slowly, over millions of years, they grew out of the weakness and became strong enough to take it. But I always thought it was a strong thing to do—to die when someone didn't love you any more. Therefore Judas is stronger than he appears. (*NOSEWORTHY stops talking and listens to guitar for a moment.*) We can imagine that there are now more people dead than are currently living. But then it was very different. There were so many more alive than dead. I mean back at the beginning of the world, when being dead was a new thing, a new idea. For a while, there were more people on earth than in heaven.

ISCARIOT stares at MARY throughout the whole scene. She alternately tries to meet and avoid his gaze. NOSEWORTHY circles table looking over the shoulders of the others as they work at their laptops.

PEEWEE: Cats think that way.

R: Shall we get back to that conversation?

NOSEWORTHY: That's what we're here for.

MARY: Is it?

K: I thought so.

NOSEWORTHY: Continue, Mizoguchi.

ISCARIOT: I can't lose my mind to the belief.

F: Is it so weak that it cannot later refuse?

MARY: It's the later refusal that creates weakness and uncertainty.

ISCARIOT: I hate that feeling.

K: Have you been feeling it lately?

ISCARIOT: No, because I haven't believed, so I've saved myself from the feeling.

PEEWEE: I still feel constant doubt.

NOSEWORTHY: Which you have been concealing from us.

ISCARIOT: If I believe, I loose myself among you. I prefer to doubt.

F: That's not so bad.

R: But don't you find yourself in the comfort and familiarity of the group?

ISCARIOT: Don't want to be.

MARY: Can't give it up.

PEEWEE: But give up the familiarity you were born into?

ISCARIOT: Give up what I was born with—my independence.

K: Like the pound or the dollar.

MARY: Were you born with it?

PEEWEE: Maybe you learned or acquired it.

R: Only to have it broken here?

K: Is it broken?

PEEWEE: ou are trying to break it.

ISCARIOT: Must you say those things?

NOSEWORTHY: It's our job.

ISCARIOT: Just don't say anything, and let me doubt in silence.

MARY: Silent doubt always becomes a scream or operatic singing.

PEEWEE: Grunge.

R: It's now so loud in the room that we cannot bear it.

K: Cover your ears. That's what I do.

ISCARIOT: Isn't that what you do all the time to maintain your group belief?!

PEEWEE: Is that why you are hearing screaming now?

ISCARIOT: I will not be taken to Funkytown!

R: You've tainted the air of belief, the very nature of …

MARY: … submission.

F: Love, devotion, and surrender.

ISCARIOT: My mind will not change. Can you break it for me? I welcome the relief of being like you. I can't break it myself. You must do it for me.

NOSEWORTHY: Okay, I'll do it.

R: If we do it, it may maim you, and you will go around limping like us.

K: Limping?

NOSEWORTHY: … But believing all the same.

ISCARIOT: You have to submit willingly.

PEEWEE: And be a pawn and a fool like you.

K: I'm not so foolish.

ISCARIOT: You don't have to believe all the time.

MARY: Small doubts turn into big ones.

ISCARIOT: That's your problem.

NOSEWORTHY: Our problem.

MARY: You can't let the doubt dissolve.

ISCARIOT: *(ISCARIOT and MARY's eyes meet.)* It cannot dissolve in the true compromise of your beautiful face.

NOSEWORTHY: This is personal and confidential, and we will not talk about it anymore!

PEEWEE: We will scream silently about it. Poetically.

ISCARIOT: Poetry only leads to disillusion; we learned that the first week.

K: That was twenty-five years ago.

R: Robert Frost, Yeats, Emily Dickinson.

ISCARIOT: Unbelievers, all.

MARY: Beautiful but useless poetry.

PEEWEE: Do you want to become a beautiful and useless poem?

K: I have been one all my life.

ISCARIOT: Well, anyway.

NOSEWORTHY: Your mind is screaming, and you must settle down.

ISCARIOT: My head is a mushroom cloud.

PEEWEE: Porcini dust.

MARY: The mushroom crumbles in the wake of its own disbelief.

ISCARIOT: Rather than being soft and supple.

PEEWEE: Hell-bent.

MARY: The easier to bend it, my dear.

NOSEWORTHY: Twisted sister, restrain yourself!

PEEWEE: Then you are not compromised.

R: Will you please stop confusing things.

MARY: I only mean to clarify.

F: You believe. You are compromised because you believe.

MARY: You believe because you are compromised.

NOSEWORTHY: Belief does not exonerate you from being compromised.

PEEWEE: It worked for Jesus.

MARY: I really believe in what we are doing.

ISCARIOT: Me too.

NOSEWORTHY: Shut up, Judas.

K: What are you doing?

NOSEWORTHY: Think of it this way: We all know what we are doing individually, but we are keeping it a secret from each other. That way no one is compromised.

ISCARIOT: How are we to work together if …

R: That's exactly how.

NOSEWORTHY: A perfect design.

R: It's design by design. Swift.

ISCARIOT: Shallow.

F: It's only design, not philosophy.

MARY: Organization of ideas, not ideas themselves.

R walks over to ISCARIOT *and looks over his shoulder at his laptop.*

K: We're just organizing?

PEEWEE: Well, I am. What are you doing?

K: What are you doing?

NOSEWORTHY: Taking notes.

R: I'm not getting eye contact.

ISCARIOT: I don't need eye contact.

K: Oh, I do.

ISCARIOT: What do you think you can see if you do look at me?

NOSEWORTHY: Okay, let's move on.

R: *(Returns to her seat.)* What are you getting?

MARY: Oh here, I have it …

K: *(Stands at attention and recites.)* Koizumi releases stress with legendary lewdness. Prime Minister Junichiro Koizumi's meeting in November last year with Greek counterpart Kostas Karamanlis raised barely a ripple in the media; but *Asahi Geino* of 3/23 says their talks bordered on the filthy, as Japan's premier let loose with the lechery those close to him say he is known for. *(Looking around.)* What are we talking about? Who are we? What are we doing here? *(Sits.)*

NOSEWORTHY: Didn't they tell you?

K: No.

ISCARIOT: Who are we, and what are we doing here?!

NOSEWORTHY: By the tone of your question it leads me to believe that we are German high school students.

K: Why do I exist?

PEEWEE: If you really existed, you wouldn't ask such a useless question.

K: You mean we're not characters? And why are you two idiots always singing?

PEEWEE and ISCARIOT: *(Looking at MARY, they sing.)* "Oh, it's such a perfect day," etc.

PEEWEE: Lemon and McHenry.

ISCARIOT: Don't you like it?

NOSEWORTHY: I hear no melody whatsoever in it.

K: Oh, I do.

ISCARIOT: You? You seem to be the last one who would be looking for a melody and wondering about those other things like, "Why do I exist?" and, "Am I a character?"

Noseworthy: We're part of a mood, a colorization, a wash.

F: Can't you just lose yourself in it, in the blinking lights, and be happy?

Iscariot: I am not going to Funkytown!

K: It's what Biggie Smalls or Hobbes said: "the war of all against all."

Iscariot: We love it, but we don't talk about it.

R: Can we change the subject?

Noseworthy: I'm sorry, but we are going to have to rewrite you.

Iscariot: *(Whispering.)* Bring it on, motherfuckers.

Noseworthy: Peewee, you start.

Peewee: Shall we get back to that conversation?

Iscariot: That's what we're here for.

Noseworthy: Continue, Mizoguchi.

Iscariot: I can't be taken in by the belief.

Peewee: No …

Iscariot: But I can give my mind up to the belief. Or lose it to the belief.

Noseworthy: Lose that.

F: Acceptance creates strength and certainty.

Iscariot: I love that feeling.

R: Feeling it lately?

Iscariot: I have believed—so I have the feeling.

Mary: I still feel constant doubt.

Noseworthy: No, no! Take that out!

Peewee: You have been concealing it from us.

Iscariot: I believe, and find myself among you.

F: Not so bad.

R: Find yourself in the comfort and familiarity of the group.

ISCARIOT: Yes.

R: Strong.

ISCARIOT: I will.

R: You are part of it.

MARY: You were born with it.

ISCARIOT: My independence?

K: Broken?

ISCARIOT: No.

PEEWEE: You are trying to break it.

F: Must you say those things?

NOSEWORTHY: It's our job.

ISCARIOT: Let me doubt out loud.

NOSEWORTHY: Always.

ISCARIOT: Always.

PEEWEE: Doubt becomes grunge.

F: The music is now so sweet in the room.

MARY: *(Rising forcefully and leaning over the table facing ISCARIOT.)* Listening to music—isn't that what you do all the time to maintain your believing thoughts?!

NOSEWORTHY: Hearing screaming now?

MARY turns her back on the table.

ISCARIOT: No.

PEEWEE: Get out!

ISCARIOT: *(Gets up and walks over to face MARY.)* My mind will change. Break it for me. The relief to be like you.

NOSEWORTHY: It may help you, and you will go around limping like us.

K: Limping, but believing?

R: Don't have to believe all the time.

MARY: Pretend once in awhile.

PEEWEE: Big doubts into small ones.

K: Frost, Yeats, Emily.

NOSEWORTHY: Believers, all.

MARY: Beautiful, useless poetry.

ISCARIOT: I want to become a beautiful and useless poem.

K: Been one all my life.

PEEWEE: Easier to bend it, dear.

MARY: Untwisted sister.

K: Worked for Jesus.

NOSEWORTHY: I really believe in what we are doing.

MARY: Hello, Judas. What are you doing?

ISCARIOT: We all know what we are doing, but no one is compromised.

R: Exactly.

ISCARIOT: Perfect design.

K: Design by design.

NOSEWORTHY: We're reorganizing.

R: I am. What are you doing?

ISCARIOT: Don't need eye contact

K: Oh, I do.

NOSEWORTHY: Move on.

R: What are you getting?

ISCARIOT: Oh, here I have it …

PEEWEE and ISCARIOT: *(Singing over track of "In the Rain," by The Dramatics.)* "I wanna go outside in the rain," etc.

ISCARIOT: Koizumi releases stress with legendary lewdness. *(Recites first verse of "Atlantis," by Donovan.)* "The continent of Atlantis was an island which lay before the great flood in the area we now call the Atlantic Ocean," etc. We are German high school students. We exist. *(Returns to seat.)*

PEEWEE: Bring it on, motherfuckers.

R: Peewee, you start.

PEEWEE: Again? How many times?

NOSEWORTHY: From the mid-section.

ISCARIOT: I'll feed you the line.

PEEWEE: *(Stands and recites.)* But *Asahi Geino* of 3/23 says talks bordered on filthy, Japan's premier, etc., and we're characters. Lennon and McCartney. *(Sits.)*

ISCARIOT: I hear melody.

K: *(Standing, yells at ISCARIOT.)* You?! You seem to be the last one who would be looking for a melody and wondering about those other things like, "Why do I exist?" and, "Am I a character?" You're part of a mood, a colorization, a wash. Can't you just lose yourself in it, in the blinking lights, and be happy?!

ISCARIOT: *(ISCARIOT stands, yelling at K.)* Why don't you take me to Funkytown?!

ISCARIOT and K: *(Yelling at each other face to face.)* It is what Biggie Smalls said about "the war of all against all!" *(They sit and face forward.)*

MARY: We love it, but we don't talk about it.

NOSEWORTHY: Do you want to change the subject?

K: Oh, I do.

R: Continue.

K: *(Looking forward, astonished.)* What a beautiful painting on the wall!!

MARY: I never noticed it.

F: It just arrived today.

MARY: Oh, I don't care.

ISCARIOT: Oh, I really like it.

MARY: Well, you would!

NOSEWORTHY: Could you explain the picture to me?

K: Do you really want me to?

R: *(Sits uncomfortably in center chair and faces back towards camera. Her face is projected on center screen. She slowly becomes more hysterical throughout the scene.)* It's rather disturbing.

MARY: Oh, I find it lovely. Please explain.

NOSEWORTHY: And please don't leave anything out.

K: *(K rises and walks to the edge of the stage. As he speaks, he points at different areas of the apparently huge painting facing them.)* Apollo's head has exploded in radiating sun rays. And this is Venus, who is in tears. She was upset that the upper gods were starting to emulate the lower classes, and not vice versa. Silently, she wails.

R: What else?

MARY: *(Pointing into the wings for the rest of the scene.)* Is that Athena? Malinche?

K: Bitch of bitch and whore of whores.

R: That is her husband, the Snowman! He's a bastard, motherfucker, moth-er, motherfucker!!

PEEWEE: And they shall reign forever and ever.

R: What did you say?!

K: *(Pointing on tiptoe.)* And these are Delilah and Samson. She has slit his neck with a silver-stringed guitar string and blinded him with a sharp-ened guitar pick plectrum.

PEEWEE: *(To R.)* Are you getting uncomfortable, dear?

R: That's okay. The man in the big Mexican hat—who is that?!

K: We don't know.

PEEWEE: What do you mean, you don't know? He's been standing there for an hour.

K: We think he's Mexican.

NOSEWORTHY: You think? Not good enough.

R: Diego Rivera?!

PEEWEE: Wrong.

R: What's her name—Frida?!!

K: Not.

R: *(Screaming.)* Montezumi?!!

NOSEWORTHY: Maybe …

K: Close enough.

NOSEWORTHY: Fact check! Quickly!

MARY faces camera. Her face is projected on center screen. ISCARIOT stands in front of the table facing audience.

MARY: Well, I want to get back to that funeral.

ISCARIOT: Well, I don't. I wasn't at that funeral.

MARY: Yes you were, and that soliloquy you gave at his funeral was so weak. I knew it was a fake. I was twelve then, and I could see you were just faking it. All that time he was in the hospital, and you never went to see him once.

ISCARIOT: He was not in the hospital, and he was never in a coma; but he died of a mysterious disease.

MARY: He knew that you were just too busy, even though you knew he was dying. He knew that, and we knew that. Why else did you think he was there? FOR his health? I went there every day.

ISCARIOT: I didn't.

MARY: And that's why we let you speak. To let you off the hook somehow. But you're not off the hook. You are the hook. We did it to forgive you. I think he forgave you at the funeral.

ISCARIOT: During the soliloquy.

MARY: It doesn't matter; you're still carrying that hook around with you because you can't forgive yourself.

ISCARIOT: Like Captain Hook.

MARY: That's why the kids call you Captain Hook. They can tell.

ISCARIOT: I went there every day.

K: (*Stands up from his seat at the table and addresses audience.*) I have appeared to go unnoticed in this group of donkeys. Disguised as a fellow donkey. But I am not a donkey. It seems to be what I am being told to be … by myself. I think. But I thought all the others talked to their own well-meaning selves about such things. But they don't. They are instead their own self-informants on the Website. I do think they are donkeys. I don't seem to see my image on the Website as my own. I don't recognize the tender parts of my face even when it is so convincing. I don't recognize myself. I thought we were remaking ourselves as a generation; but I look around at our little herd of donkeys and I see nothing but children

of the corn. I tried to get on the train to Kansas City; but they've can-
celled the route, so I guess I'll stay. I don't know why I'm telling this to
the Website, since it will blow back to me. Maybe I am a donkey. *(Sits.)*

PEEWEE: Why did you reveal that? What are you talking about? Yourself ?

MARY: Now we have to get rid of you.

K: Oh, I don't care.

R: Where will you go?

K: Oh, I don't know.

MARY: You know.

ISCARIOT: Well, I know. Your ass will be so uploaded that your reputation
will be destroyed.

K: My reputation as a donkey?

NOSEWORTHY: You'll be sent out.

K: Where's that?

F: Sent down, flat-lined.

PEEWEE: De-incarnated.

MARY: Re-incarcerated.

K: Dead?

PEEWEE: Yes, but we know that paradise after death is eternally
nonexistent.

K: You mean we don't get lifted?

PEEWEE: You're working here, and you still believe that you get lifted?

NOSEWORTHY: Get a grip.

ISCARIOT: Boy, are you in for a letdown.

R: Why did you confess all that?

K: It was true.

ISCARIOT: So what!

R: You're only supposed to put fluff reports on the Website. Everyone knows that.

PEEWEE: It's like confession—you just make up some small infraction. You never tell the truth.

MARY: You never even tell the truth to yourself.

K: I thought you were supposed to.

F: But where is the poetry in all the fluff?

PEEWEE: The fluff is the poetry.

K: I can't believe that!

NOSEWORTHY: ... And now you will never get lifted.

ISCARIOT: I thought you could remake yourself, but I suppose not.

NOSEWORTHY: Now there is no possibility in rekindling. I'll get coffee. (Leaves.)

F: I think it's time for you to go.

K: I'll wait.

MARY: And how dare you call us monkeys?!

ISCARIOT: Donkeys.

PEEWEE: Same.

MARY: It' s not.

ISCARIOT: Worse!

F: Donkeys implies no intellectual ability at all.

K: Exactly.

ISCARIOT: Monkeys have no emotions.

R: How could you reveal such a hostility when we put up with all your inadequacies and—

ISCARIOT:—let you slide by.

K: I let you slide by. While I played the dummy.

PEEWEE: Only a dummy would have put that up on the site.

R: It's only internal.

F: What about Miss Noseworthy? She'll report it.

PEEWEE: The bitch don't have to know.

NOSEWORTHY: *(Returning to his chair.)* The bitch knows! She was designed that way.

R: Now listen, dummy!

NOSEWORTHY: Okay, donkeys! How could you let things deteriorate to such a low level of name-calling?! The total abandonment of your God-given characters.

R: … Your personal directives. This is disastrous to the process. We are going to have to clear the entire site and start over again.

K: I wish I knew what we were doing. I did so wish to be a character.

NOSEWORTHY: There, you see? He is recanting his former recalcitrant stance. A few re-corrections, and he'll be fine.

PEEWEE: He won't have to be lifted from the face of the earth. He remains part of the regeneration.

MARY: But I think he should be removed. He's dangerous.

K: I will not be taken to Donkeytown!

R: Could you just refract that into something else so we can restore our stability on this very rocky—

ISCARIOT:—donkey ride.

PEEWEE: It worked for Jesus.

F: That poor donkey regretted waking up that morning for the rest of its life!

NOSEWORTHY: And so will you.

ISCARIOT: That poor donkey.

NOSEWORTHY: Now, back to order. Take your places and your positions.

K: Take me to the river!!

PEEWEE: Why is he still here if he did such a thing?

NOSEWORTHY: Continue.

K: They will eventually give into the weaknesses of their minds. Donkeys always do.

ISCARIOT: They will end up on the other side.

K: What other side?

ISCARIOT: Oh, don't start with the dummy questions again!

PEEWEE: Whatever other side there is.

MARY: The other side of nowhere.

PEEWEE: … Or just nowhere.

K: The other side of us.

ISCARIOT: The communal ecstasy of donkey thought.

R: What do donkeys think about?

K: Ask yourself.

PEEWEE: You express these sentiments, yet you never pay for them.

MARY: What are you thinking about?

ISCARIOT: Nothing.

NOSEWORTHY: Can we all just stop thinking for a minute!

R: I think we've lost the subject again.

F: Oh, that's okay.

PEEWEE: It's not.

NOSEWORTHY: Can we please get back to the subject?!

MARY: Someone keeps changing it.

R: What are you think about, K?

K: Nothing.

PEEWEE: Yes you are.

K: I'm not.

NOSEWORTHY: What are you doing?

K: Just sitting and not thinking.

F: And what are you doing?

ISCARIOT: *(Looking at MARY.)* I'm thinking that I'm not a character; I'm a directive. I am nobody; but I am something. But I am in ecstasy. Ecstatic.

R: What time is it?

K: Eight-thirty-one P.M.

NOSEWORTHY: Please stop interrupting, and get back to the point!

R: *(R and F embrace.)* Will you please stop talking about that funeral? I feel sorry for her; but someone said that you get cancer from feeling sorry for others. It's weak to do that. Such was the fate of the concubines in the Forbidden Purple City.

NOSEWORTHY: Who are we? I have the new directive: You two can sing the entrance hymn. Read.

ISCARIOT: As you know, generations generate much more quickly now. As we know, every two years there is a new generation, a new system of thought and being.

MARY: We were created by the last one, but are so advanced that we think we created ourselves.

R: We have created ourselves and are creating ourselves. We are as distanced from our forebears of two years as they were from their grandparents a century before.

F: They are standing in the shadows of love.

PEEWEE: We are as far from them as they were from the Cro Mags.

K: Hardly connected.

MARY: Developed into another species perhaps?

PEEWEE: Like the retarded.

ISCARIOT: Zits on the face of God.

PEEWEE: If there was a God, it would be us.

NOSEWORTHY: Experience the divine.

K: Are we some kind of concubines?

MARY: I had so wanted to be a character, but not that.

F: It's not about characters.

PEEWEE: We know characters are not believable.

ISCARIOT: They lie worse than real people.

NOSEWORTHY: A character is a meditation on itself, so let's get over that right now.

F: Just enjoy the show.

PEEWEE: So we're just wandering voices trying to connect to disembodied bodies?

ISCARIOT: I don't hear any voices but ours.

K: Oh, I do.

MARY: That has been my struggle for the last ten minutes; but my struggle did not last very long.

PEEWEE: Now I am a bright vermillion orange orangutan chewing papyrus.

R: It's just reordering pieces that have already been made.

ISCARIOT: Us.

PEEWEE: Lego blocks.

NOSEWORTHY: They're my favorite toys.

ISCARIOT: *(Grabbing* NOSEWORTHY *violently by the face.)* It's not a toy; it's a processor, a teaching device, a system for teaching conformity!

K: If you get to know the shape of the pieces well enough and how they fit together, you will succeed.

R: There is nothing complex in putting it together like orangutans.

K: Are we the monkeys, or the pieces?

MARY: Both are needed.

R: The monkeys make some variations; but they repeat over and over the action of fitting them together in the same way.

F: I am not a monkey!

MARY: That is the voice of hope.

PEEWEE: We are animals.

MARY: Anthill, beehive, pasture.

R: We have nice big leather boots.

K: Made out of OUR cow relatives and made by OUR Chinese relatives who are distantly related.

MARY: But of a lowER status, which is why we wear them to prove, to reiterate everyday our own superiority and their inferiority.

F: But I don't want to be a cow!

R: You are so fearful.

F: I don't want to be a cow!

PEEWEE: If you are afraid of being one, then you already are one.

NOSEWORTHY: That's what makes them cows.

K: I can't keep up with all this.

PEEWEE: That's because you are also a cow.

K: I thought I was a donkey.

NOSEWORTHY: Cows can't understand all this and admit it, and so they are allowed to go out to rapturous pastures …

F: … And eventually be made into boots and stew.

PEEWEE: … And saddles.

MARY: And then they are ridden.

F: Re-morphed, re-transmuted into positive, useful objects.

MARY: (*At live camera, face on screen.*) After that job interview with Mr. Noseworthy, I bumped into Cathy. She wasn't glad to see me. Very cold, hard eyes. She never did really become a writer. I had wanted so much to be a character and not just sit here and talk. I had wanted to become the replicant of a person born in the mind of somebody else. To be made up by someone else. I wanted to become a creation in the mind of someone else. I wanted that warm, cozy feeling like you get when you drink red wine and listen to heavy metal music.

PEEWEE: We are going forward. That is our aim: to go forward.

F: That is our purpose, that is who we are.

K: We are a forward motion. That's exciting.

ISCARIOT: We are movement without thought.

MARY: Glory without sound.

R: Cat scratch fever.

F: It's a kind of fever ecstasy.

PEEWEE: We are blowing in the wind. Now I understand that song.

K replaces MARY *in front of camera and on center screen. Except for K, all hold hands across the length of the table, eyes closed.*

NOSEWORTHY: As you can see, we are restructuring everything pursuant to the bailout of K.

R: But he will now be the stupid one.

PEEWEE: But how could the stupid one have the urge to leave? Doesn't that indicate not stupid?

MARY: It only indicates uncooperativeness, revulsion at the order of things.

F: Personal revulsion towards at us.

R: Why? We are only trying to collaborate.

K: How could I have been so stupid even when I didn't realize it?

NOSEWORTHY: And now you will pay for it.

K: I want to come back into the group.

MARY: No.

K: But I don't want to be just an idea.

F: Isn't that enough?

K: A person is nothing. The idea is stronger. The person will dissolve into the idea. Who did you say I was again?

PEEWEE: No one.

K: Oh, good. Thanks for clearing that up.

R: Can we get back, please, to the forward thrust?

Iscariot: If am not a character—personality—person—then why I am I feeling?

Mary: Feeling what?

R: Only feel the forward movement.

F: That's all you need.

R: Have we all stopped thinking?

Mary: Yes.

Noseworthy: Good.

K: What are you thinking about?

F: Nothing.

K: Are you sure?

Noseworthy: Concentrate.

Iscariot: I am free. The ecstasy of communal concentration. Donkeys often don't know why they are doing; but we do. What are you doing ?

R: I'm supposed to keep the show going.

Noseworthy: I follow the rules; I don't make them. It's me, Miss Noseworthy.

Peewee: I lie.

K: I give up.

F: I try to find goodness and intelligence in everyone.

Peewee: I try to fuck everything up for the fun of it.

Mary: I truly believe in changing all this, even if I have to introduce false information to do it. I am the only one here who believes in anything.

K: The rest are donkeys. I look at them and I see little donkey faces bobbing up and down in front of the trough of ecstasy.

NOSEWORTHY: You should try it sometime.

K: I really have no idea what is going on at all. I just try to keep up. I don't even know how I got this part, even though they tell me it is not a part.

ISCARIOT: I didn't get to say who I am.

MARY: I had just wanted to be a beautiful tragic character like Anna Karenina and jump in front of a train.

PEEWEE: I'll push you

F: It's more beautiful to jump.

K: Oh, I don't think so.

PEEWEE: Oh, I do.

NOSEWORTHY: Can we please get back to the subject again?

R: Can you check those facts, please?

F: Anna Karenina—Tolstoy.

K: Train?

PEEWEE: Strike the author's name, it's not important.

R: I don't know how I'm going to explain this conversation.

NOSEWORTHY: All conversations must be reviewed and fact-checked for inference and intent.

F: We've lost the thread again.

R: Please locate it.

F: Oh, yes. Wandering mind. Lost train of thought.

MARY: Anna lost her train of thought and—

NOSEWORTHY: Yes, that's it.

R: We went off track. That's a good explanation for Anna K.

K: Do you mean me, K?

NOSEWORTHY: We make them all work in the attic, where they belong. It's what they deserve, and that way they realize that and stay up there and be grateful for it.

R: Will you please stop trying to inject your personal feelings?

NOSEWORTHY: I don't have any. I told you, I am not even a character.

F: Has everyone stopped thinking with their eyes closed?

PEEWEE: Yes. *(All release hands.)*

MARY: I want to be a character. I want to be somebody.

K: No, you don't.

ISCARIOT: Can I please explain my directive to you?

NOSEWORTHY: Who gave you that directive?

ISCARIOT: I can't remember.

F: What matters is not who gave it to you, but that you received it.

MARY: *(To ISCARIOT.)* I am not in love with you.

PEEWEE: Thanks FOR CLARIFYING that.

K: I wasn't paying attention; but all I know is that's what I have to do.

ISCARIOT: Or …

NOSEWORTHY: Or else what?

K: I don't know; but I'd better do it, because that other person behind me will tell me what to do. Or it won't be happy.

R: Is it a person, or a character?

K: It has all the ideas. I just receive them. And let me tell you what she told me. I am the front part of her mind, the most shallow and superficial; but I do all the dumb stuff.

PEEWEE: Like what?

K: Like this. And talking to you other donkeys in the stable.

NOSEWORTHY: Please, let's get back to work.

K: We have to end somewhere.

ISCARIOT: I don't think we're allowed to see that.

K: I see it. I see a cold book sitting on the street that must have fallen out of a car.

PEEWEE: Or been thrown out.

MARY: It fell purposely, like Anna K.

F: Will you please stop talking about her?

K: She was a victory of form over nature.

ISCARIOT: Trash that.

F: The whole Karenina thing again?

R: Our trash will be full of all those references, and it will become problematic. They will think we have a reading club down here.

NOSEWORTHY: Did you find that youth molecule? Could you send it to me, please?

F: Try just to enjoy the day.

PEEWEE: You've become scary and weird.

R: Is that our directive? Scary and weird? I think not.

ISCARIOT: No.

NOSEWORTHY: Then get it off the screen.

K: Is this some kind of a show?

ISCARIOT and MARY face each other at opposite ends of the long table. NOSEWORTHY sits in center chair facing camera. Each face is projected on the screen live.

ISCARIOT: Who were you talking to?

MARY: No one.

ISCARIOT: Yes you were, I saw you.

MARY: I was talking to myself.

ISCARIOT: The little Druid you were talking to in there, who is that?

MARY: Miss Noseworthy. She's new. I'm trying to find out what her gig is.

ISCARIOT: Don't do it. You'll become compromised. By doing that you are robbing a donkey to pay a monkey!

MARY: Or something like that.

ISCARIOT: Well, it's got to stop!

MARY: How can I stop it?

NOSEWORTHY: I've had enough of the anti-semantics, and I want you guys to play by the rules. Follow the rules, or it will be the water cannon! I'm not going to say it again! Divorce yourselves from consequence and do the job!

ISCARIOT: I really wish you would keep your transgender friends out of here.

MARY: It's her job.

ISCARIOT: Then keep her out of the bathrooms. She's nothing but a dilettante, a goat herder.

MARY: Those were the job requirements.

ISCARIOT: "To the East, Africa was a neighbor, across a short strait of sea miles. The great Egyptian age is but a remnant of the Atlantian culture." And Judas wept.

MARY: Will you please stop reciting that poem; it's making me sick to the heart.

ISCARIOT: I learned it from Jesus, and I believed it, and then it never happened.

MARY: It's a stupid poem. I taught it to him as a child.

ISCARIOT: Then he was stupid to learn it, and so was I.

NOSEWORTHY: Please explain the donkey reference.

PEEWEE: It's their soul, it's their language, it's their gut. It's all they have. There isn't anything else. It's them. All they know thru and thru. It's all they have. It's not like they can go to Bethlehem and reinvent themselves—*quelle horreur!* There's nowhere else for them to go in their minds. The world inside is the world outside. So they stay and defend what they are. What's theirs. Not because they love it so much, but because it's all they perceive and believe they are. If they lose that, they lose everything.

R: I am not traveling with this puppet show!

MARY: Unfortunately and unbelievably, our group happened to be the best, the most superficial, the most plastic, and the most perfect in its form and expression. And with the sincerity and passion of our superficiality, we actually had a power.

K: (*Stands up and walks to front of stage, addressing audience.*) They in their expression seemed to believe the most in what they were saying, no matter how vapid the content. They were so wrapped up in the expression that they actually really believed in it, and believed that they believed in it. And they believed in the truth of their false expression. Stupid, you might say, to be so fooled by your own passionate belief in the vapid. (*Turns towards performers.*) How could something so transparently insincere be put across so sincerely? Is it dangerous to do this?

PEEWEE: In your donkey soul, you know it is.

NOSEWORTHY: Fact check!

R: It can't be us you're talking about.

K: In your donkey soul, it is! Are we some kind of mental concubines in the service of—

The calmly bewildered face of a young man appears on the center screen.

R: I want to play you the last known directive of our last coordinator.

PEEWEE: Jesus?

F: Is that him?

K: That was fifty years ago. He doesn't look like the pictures at all.

NOSEWORTHY: Dudes, get back to work.

ISCARIOT: He was the one who died in the fishpond in Swahililand.

NOSEWORTHY: Quiet, Mr. Iscariot. You know who it is.

MARY: Why do we have to look at this?

R: It's scary and weird.

ISCARIOT: Are you scared?

PEEWEE: Poor cow.

NOSEWORTHY: It's just research. Anyone can look it up.

PEEWEE: It's not so scary.

R: It is scary, and I won't look.

MARY: You will look and not be scared. *(She looks away.)*

NOSEWORTHY: Okay, enough! Back to work, dudes.

K: He's a mess, poor thing. We never should have abandoned him.

F: Wait, he's talking …

PEEWEE: You were supposed to find a common ground; but you didn't, did you? How are you?

JESUS: I have to lie down again. I'm spinning. I cut myself on my own tongue. Water came out of my skin. I cried. Everything went from blue to pink. I'm afraid …

PEEWEE: Did you hear that? He's afraid, like the cow and the donkey. But that's an old way of thinking. What's wrong?

JESUS: I don't understand the space, how to navigate it. So I return to memory one last time.

R: What is it really, JESUS ?

JESUS: We don't have names here.

K: Oh, we do … Who is Goldfinch? His pupils are dilated. Is he on a drug? Didn't I see you at that funeral? Didn't I?

JESUS: No ghosts, please!

PEEWEE: I told you not to get on that donkey! We could have saved you! We had to rewrite everything for you!

JESUS: … In your own mind. I think this is self-explanatory. First the mess of reality. Then the cleaned-up version. A beautiful Judas kiss.

K: From our illustrious childhood we were taught to find meanings in things and reasons for things.

JESUS: To look for cracks and put them back together in a way that they will not fall apart!

K: Okay! … From the age of nothing … And now you tell me it is not always possible?

JESUS: Not in anyone's lifetime.

ISCARIOT: If you should ever get that old. That is almost—

JESUS: No ghosts, please.

R: How could that be?

JESUS: No ghosts, please … Please!

NOSEWORTHY: By that we mean the Website. First the memory.

JESUS: No ghosts, please.

PEEWEE: Then the excuse. First the truth. Then the lie. Then the truth.

JESUS: Then the lie. Then a kiss goodnight. Compatibility … Consequently, re-clarification. *(Pauses and stops talking.)*

R: Say something, Jesus!

PEEWEE: You see what happened to him? His mind is playing tricks on him, poor thing. Mary, you aren't saying much.

NOSEWORTHY: Shut it off.

K: All his work. He worked so hard. What became of it? Where did it lead? Did it ever mean anything to anyone? We never should have abandoned him.

ISCARIOT: I'm glad I did. Otherwise I would have ended up like you.

K: I only count seven.

PEEWEE: I see twelve.

ISCARIOT: So do I.

R: Then if you do, I do.

MARY: There aren't twelve.

F: There are twelve.

NOSEWORTHY: Could you delete him, please?

PEEWEE *hits a key on his computer and* JESUS's *face disappears from screen.*

MARY: *(On center screen.)* I was looking at them with innocent eyes. The innocent eye is essentially the pinhole through which one perceives. What the eye focuses on has as much to do with physical as well as mental processes occurring on both sides of it. I thought it was as simple as that. I thought I could change them because my belief was so strong. But you can never change a donkey into a monkey without bloodying the waters. I was willing to do that, but now I have been worn down by my own constant toleration of their uncertainty. I was willing to kill them to change them. To rip out their innocent eyes. To make them give up the funk. But it would have been like killing innocent animals. I have been worn down by my constant uncertainty of their toleration of me. It's stronger than my belief in my own ideals. My work was all about hope and joy and positive things, and how everything was going to be all right; and then they all went on to become donkeys. And me, a donkey killer. I am nothing but cold hard cash, and nothing can make me warm again.

F: *(On center screen.)* Mary? I hadn't seen her in years; but I noticed she had a hard cold look in her eyes. Her powder blue, blue eyes had turned to steel, and they cut right through me. Sharply. I realized that she had finally given up her friendly tone. She was always so friendly; but it had turned harsh and suspicious. After what we did to her son, I don't blame her.

MARY: *(Onstage.)* I had so wanted to be a character.

K: But you are, Mary.

MARY: Am I Mary?

K: You were the only one that believed in anything.

PEEWEE: Your affair with Iscariot was an unfortunate backstage indiscretion for which your son-god never forgave you. And so he left you in the mortal world with the rest of us traitors.

MARY slaps PEEWEE.

PEEWEE and ISCARIOT: *(Singing.)* "Oh, it's such a perfect day," etc.

MARY: So I am a character after all. How satisfying to have been someone.

K: It's better than what we have to endure—being mouthpieces for the doubts of the Nazarene.

MARY: At least you get to sing.

K: The only one who got to sing was Iscariot, who sang to his Mafia friends!

MARY: Now my poor son is—

NOSEWORTHY:—living in Switzerland. We know it.

F: Okay, fine, they didn't kill him, but almost!

Mary: How would you like to be put to death by your own believers?

Peewee: They would be the most efficient.

R: What we are after is not death, but efficiency.

F: Efficiency is pure beauty.

Mary: Ungodliness.

Peewee: Don't talk to me about God and your failed attempt to be Its mother.

F: True, it did fail; but it was a good try.

Mary: I've been left with a wooden legacy, a half-myth, a Mexican hat dance.

Noseworthy: And you guys did not do your job!

Mary: You canned out, and the thing we worked so hard for fell apart. You lost the rapture.

K: We were weak as donkeys.

Mary: *(Yanks Peewee by the collar.)* I had the other five donkeys killed. Vengeance was mine. I let the rest of you live out your stupid donkey lives. *(Releases Peewee with a violent shove.)* Twelve minus five is—

K: —seven. But Jesus, is his soul really free?

Mary: Mine is not. It still belongs to him.

R: You saw what he turned into at the first taste of fear and failure.

Iscariot: He was weak! We did all the work for him, and when it came his turn, he let us down!

Peewee: And you lost the passion I never had.

K: All his search for beauty has left him. He has been institutionalized.

Peewee: Who was in that casket at his burial?

K: His autographed copy of the teachings of the Buddha.

PEEWEE: And your dog.

K: *(Jumps up sobbing.)* When they rolled away the stone, they was gone, of course! *(Sits down and sobs into his hands.)*

MARY: I cannot contemplate the dementiated state of his Swiss-charred mind. I can't be taken in by the belief, give my mind up to the belief. I hate that feeling.

ISCARIOT: *(Rising.)* I love it!

MARY: *(Rising.)* Mr. Iscariot, you have been concealing something. I sensed a weakness in the room; but I had no idea it was you. Fifty years ago I lovingly put my baby into a cradle, and you have crushed it.

ISCARIOT: If you don't love me, I will die like a donkey on a train track!

MARY: Karenina?

ISCARIOT: Yes.

MARY: *(Turning her back to ISCARIOT.)* Go for it.

PEEWEE and ISCARIOT: *(Singing.)* "Oh, it's such a perfect day," etc.

NOSEWORTHY: *(Standing at center of table.)* Okay, as you now all know, we are the twelve selected as followers.

K: But I don't want to be a flower. I had so wanted to be a character, something recognizable, someone you could recognize.

PEEWEE: You are unrecognizable.

R: And we will all be killed.

K: What's all this about—a funeral?

ISCARIOT: Our dear friend and his confidante, Magdalena Karenina.

MARY: The soliloquy.

F: *(To MARY.)* You've always had a holier-than-thou.

MARY: For good reason.

PEEWEE: I don't believe you are the mother of Jesus.

MARY: Please don't sit in his chair.

K: We are seven.

NOSEWORTHY: There are twelve here.

R: Count. One, two, three, etc.—twelve. So you must follow the path we have set for ourselves.

PEEWEE: But the power and the glory …

R: It will be but long gone after we are gone.

K: But we were going to rewrite everything.

PEEWEE: Again?

NOSEWORTHY: Gospel and verse; but you won't be here to read it.

R: Okay, let's see … He left on the donkey …

NOSEWORTHY: Peewee, could you go to Rome tonight?

F: I wanted to go to Rome.

R: He must go and go alone. And then be hung upside down on a cross.

PEEWEE: I don't really need to go.

K: What's-his-name left the brunch on a bicycle.

F: They took him away on a donkey.

MARY: I don't think I like this story. It's so degrading.

R: Okay, just put that he took a donkey ride into the city.

NOSEWORTHY: And after he left the brunch—

R: Supper.

NOSEWORTHY: Okay, supper—

F:—he was taken away to the … hospital.

K: We know he skipped out to Switzerland.

MARY: After you …

R: … we …

K: … abandoned him.

F: Poor Magdalena, her legs were so thin.

ISCARIOT: … And I am getting the hell out of here.

NOSEWORTHY: There will have to be some sort of funeralization.

ISCARIOT: You can roll away the stone yourself.

F: Her legs were so thin …

R: Those unfortunate things you said about Marymag will have to be stricken from the record.

NOSEWORTHY: JESUS has left the house.

R: There have been complications.

ISCARIOT: We'd better split. We'll be implicated.

NOSEWORTHY: Someone clean up that tabouli; it's all over the place.

R: Grab the wine before it goes stale.

ISCARIOT: It's turned to urine.

NOSEWORTHY: Water! Fact check and rewrite!

R: So we will unwrite ourselves.

F: We were just having a meeting discussing …

K: I'm sorry, but I haven't been able to control myself.

PEEWEE: You will learn; but it won't save you from your eventual flaying.

R: We will erase everything before us and lay out the future of our plans for the world.

K: In pure, crushed, light blue, lovely velvet.

F: This could get messy; but we won't be around to have to clean it up.

PEEWEE: But we will rewrite the memory of us, and we'll live on in other peoples' memories, even though we'll be dead.

R: Okay, we've just been having a meeting about interpretation, funeral design, and personal politics.

PEEWEE: With snacks, dynamite, and Anna Karenina.

R: We had all better change our identities to men; that way it will be less sexual.

NOSEWORTHY: I don't mind.

ISCARIOT: Are we women?

R: Some kind of moral hermaphrodites.

PEEWEE: God's dirty underwear.

NOSEWORTHY: Okay, twelve men discussing in a room, business meeting, cultural activities.

R: Have we covered our tracks?

K: But remember, we aren't trying to fool anyone. We are trying to maintain the truth of it all.

PEEWEE: I just don't think it's going to go anywhere.

R: Somehow I wonder if you really are with us, Judas.

ISCARIOT: Does anyone have change for a thirty?

NOSEWORTHY: We will all meet again several years later for phase two. Fact check!

ISCARIOT and MARY sit in front of camera. They appear on center screen together, as ISCARIOT speaks into her ear.

ISCARIOT: The continent of Japan was an island that lay, before the Great Flood, in the area we now call the Atlantic Ocean.

MARY: Stop it.

ISCARIOT: So great an area of land that from her western shores those mutilated sailors journeyed to the South and the North Asias with ease in their ships with tainted sails.

MARY: "It's like seeing a garden at night in which certain parts are lit up so brightly that we can distinguish each blade of grass, each minute insect, each nuance of color—while the rest of the garden and the tidal wave that threatens it remain in darkness."

ISCARIOT: To the east, Mexico was a neighbor across a short strait of sea miles.

MARY: Please, I can't hear it anymore.

ISCARIOT: The great Egyptian age is but a remnant of the American culture.

MARY: It can't be true.

ISCARIOT: "The antediluvian kings colonized the world."

MARY: "All the dogs who play in the mythological dramas in all legends from all lands were from fair Atlantis."

ISCARIOT: No, they weren't.

MARY: No, we were not.

ISCARIOT: Knowing his fate, JESUS sent out ships to all corners of the Earth. On board were the Twelve: the poet, the physician, the farmer, the clown, the scientist, the donkey …

MARY: Please …

ISCARIOT: … the Mizoguchi, the drunkard, the cow, the magician, Iscariot, Miss Noseworthy, and all the other so-called gods of our legends—though gods we were not. And as the donkeys of our time choose to remain blind … "Let us rejoice, and let us sing and dance and ring in the new."

K softly strums electric guitar.

MARY: … And I saw her thirty years later, and she was beautiful, empty, pure, evacuated of all desire.

F: But I'm not like that at all. I am full of everything, and I hate her. Who knows what she thinks about me? Probably not much. I wonder if she knows about the funeral, or the cancer I got from not feeling sorry enough for wounded animals and weak people.

K: And I am sorry about your thorn-stuffed heart.

F: It's okay.

MARY: That's okay; but at least here and now, for this moment, you'll be worth something, be something, someone. We'll at least see the purity of our soulessness, and that has to be a true beauty of some kind. The perfection one sees in a donkey's eye. And we'll just sit here and accept it, and be beautiful and empty and accept it.

NOSEWORTHY: Sing, you guys.

K: And JESUS said: "We are building a world inside a world. And my heart was stuffed with happiness." What does it mean?

MARY: It's a poem; it doesn't have to mean anything. It only has to expand the universe. That's its reason for being.

K: What about me?

MARY: You'll mean something when you say it.

ISCARIOT: Say it, and you'll be stronger than dirt, stronger than the black chocolate filth of truth. The singer becomes the song. Isn't that enough? Say it and find out.

K: In the after-light, the after-bite of heaven, flaming-lipped devils–in-waiting, we soared.

About the Author

JOHN JESURUN is a playwright, director, and designer living in New York. Early in his career he worked on The Dick Cavett Show, producing shows with John and Mackenzie Phillips, John Hammond Sr., Odetta, and Tito Puente. In 1982 at the Pyramid Club in the East Village he began work on his groundbreaking and Bessie Award-winning serial play *Chang In A Void Moon*, now in its sixtieth episode. He has also created over twenty-five new works that include the media trilogy of *Deep Sleep* (Obie Award), *White Water*, and *Black Maria*, in addition to *Philoktetes*, *Everything That Rises Must Converge*, and *Faust/How I Rose*. His work has been presented at numerous venues, in the U.S. at La MaMa, the Kitchen, the Walker Arts Center, Soho Rep., BAM, the Wexner Center, and Spoleto USA, and abroad at the National Theatre of Mexico, Berliner Festspielhaus, Mickery Theater, Vienna Festival, and Kyoto Performing Arts Center. His directing credits range from Harry Partch's opera *Delusion of the Fury* to music video for Jeff Buckley. Jesurun is a 1996 MacArthur Fellow, and he has also received Guggenheim and Rockefeller Foundation fellowships. He has taught at Goethe University/Frankfurt, Justus Liebig University/Giessen, DASARTS/Amsterdam, Tokyo University, Kyoto University of Art and Design, Eugene Lang College/The New School, New York University, and Bard College. He is a graduate of the Philadelphia College of Art and Yale University.